Confessions

of a

Grinder

My first-person account of competing in the America's
Cup as a grinder on board the 12-meter *USA* from the St.
Francis Yacht Club, back when the America's Cup was
really really cool, 1986-87, Fremantle, Australia

SHARK PRESS

Confessions of a Grinder

My first-person account of competing in the America's Cup as a grinder on board the 12-meter *USA* from the St. Francis Yacht Club, back when the America's Cup was really really cool, 1986-87, Fremantle, Australia

Brad Alan Lewis

BY BRAD ALAN LEWIS

ASSAULT ON LAKE CASITAS

WANTED: ROWING COACH

LIDO FOR TIME: 14:39

THE LAST CAR IN THE PARKING LOT

DEMON BEAN - THE GREAT COFFEE WAR OF PACIFIC PALISADES

WALKING TOWARDS THUNDER

THE IDIOT YEARS

A FINE BALANCE - DOCUMENTARY ON DVD

CONFESSIONS OF A GRINDER

ISBN - 13: 978-1469944005

ISBN - 10: 1469944006

CONTACT INFO THROUGH www.bradalanlewis.com

CONFESSIONS OF A GRINDER

Prologue: Message in a Box

I returned from a long run this evening and saw the green light flashing on my message machine: "Brad, this is Bruce Epke. I was wondering if you'd like to come up to San Francisco to do a little sailing with us on the 12-meter. We need a grinder. Let me know if you're interested."

I didn't know anything about grinding, and the last time I had sailed was on a Hobie Cat fifteen years ago, but I was definitely interested.

Two days after I received Bruce's short message the fiscal end of my southern California life was reduced to a few checks crammed into envelopes to satisfy Visa, Amex, Shell and MasterCard. Without a real job or a wife or any serious outstanding debts, I was able to attempt this adventure on short notice. Not too many citizens of this urban paradise can pack up in a few days and leave for an undefined length of time for a job that promised no financial reward. I was lucky.

I earned that freedom on August 5, 1984, at Lake Casitas, the site of the Los Angeles Olympic rowing venue. With a very tough partner named Paul Enquist from Seattle, we nudged our double scull ahead of the Belgian's double scull with roughly five strokes until the finish. We won the Olympic gold medal, waved from the victory platform, shouted cheers to our families, stood ramrod straight while they played the national anthem. We were the first Americans to win the double scull event in fifty-two years, and surprisingly we were the only American men to win a rowing gold medal at the 1984 Olympiad. It was a great day. The morning after we won I went surfing at 56th Street in Newport Beach.

For thirteen years I had lived within a rowing prison, and while I loved the first ten or eleven years of confinement, I eventually started to get restless. Rowing around Newport Harbor six mornings a week and another four afternoons became unbearably tedious. I needed something new. I could think of no better adventure than 12-meter, America's Cup sailing to fulfill that desire.

I wanted to attempt this sailing adventure for another reason: to prove that I could handle a tough, long-term, team environment. Through rowing I had been labeled a loner, "the moody and resentful Californian" according to author David Halberstam in his book *The Amateurs*. But I strongly disagreed with that generalization. I was capable of being a team player, and I welcomed a chance to prove it. Surviving a year in an America's Cup syndicate would be the ultimate test, especially since a novice grinder is far down on the syndicate's hierarchy.

The offer to go sailing with Bruce was not completely unexpected. Bruce and I had been trapped in Tampa, Florida, at a grueling Olympic rowing training camp in early 1984. On our one and only afternoon of freedom during the two-week struggle, we drove across the long bridge to the St. Petersburg Yacht Club in a rented Camaro to inspect firsthand the yachts lining the docks. The yachts were here, Bruce told me, in preparation for another leg of the prestigious SORC, Southern Ocean Racing Circuit. Along with being a champion rower, Bruce was a veteran of the 1983 America's Cup and many other big boat regattas, including the SORC. As we drew near St. Petersburg he became more and more excited. His heart obviously belonged in the sailing arena and not in rowing.

We took our time walking up and down the dock, studying the wild-looking, rakish craft. Bruce introduced me to his old sailing friends, telling them proudly that he was in the process of trying out for the Olympic team. But he looked longingly at the boats, especially at a ninety-foot, ultra-sleek beauty named Boomerang, on which he had formerly crewed.

On the drive back to Tampa I told Bruce to call me after this Olympic mess was over if he ever heard of a crewing position that could be filled by someone long on enthusiasm and short on experience—someone like me. He didn't call for two years, and I'd almost forgotten having asked him to remember me. Bruce had not forgotten.

Three days after I received Bruce's message I loaded my pickup truck with a duffel bag full of clothes, a portable computer, and a surfboard and left for San Francisco. The surfboard was destined never to touch northern California waters, but over the next year I wore out the computer.

My only passenger for the long drive was Jack London's *Sea Wolf*, which I had rented from Books-on-Tape. I learned a fair amount about life at sea from this century-old book, but it did not prepare me for what lay ahead: the tension of competition, the storm-driven wild outings off San Francisco and Fremantle, the interminable boredom of boat work, the pure unadulterated fun of sharing these moments with my mates.

I left home on Thursday, February 20, 1986.

PART I: ENTER THE NOVICE SAILOR

1
Arriving

I pulled into the St. Francis Yacht Club parking lot around noon on Friday. From the sidewalk above the marina I could see two sleek sailboats, one on each side of a long skinny dock. Yes, those are 12-meters, I thought to myself. No doubt about it. Their Spartan topsides cleaned of the slightest projection confirmed that they were not cruising yachts. I knew the look of a 12-meter from my ten thousand sightseeing tours around Newport Bay. My old training ground was home to a former America's Cup contender named Newsboy.

With a dozen men on each boat working like aquatic pit crews, I was fairly sure I had come to the right place, but which boat was the USA? Bruce had told me on the phone that the Chicago syndicate was also based at the St. Francis,

11

and I asked a man who was standing along the railing, with twenty other midday spectators, which of the two yachts was the USA. I didn't want to go applying for my grinder job on the wrong boat. "The one that says 'Pacific Telesis' on the side is the USA" he said. We talked for a few seconds, and then I walked down the steep ramp that led to the dock.

The whole 12-meter name game was confusing at first: a corporation whose sole business is to win the America's Cup is called a syndicate. The syndicate based in San Francisco, to which I was applying for a crew job, was the Golden Gate Challenge. They had raised some money and built a 12-meter named USA. But this USA 12-meter was only a practice boat. The real 12-meter that the Golden Gate Challenge intended to race in Fremantle was still being designed. Most syndicates owned at least two 12-meters, one for practice and one for racing. The first USA, the one I was looking for, was nicknamed Evolutionary-1 or E-1.

I tried to look cool and ready, like hot grinder material, as I approached the USA. I was dressed in black Levis, a pair of blue Docksides, and an In-and-Out Burger T-shirt. The night before, I had shaved off my beard, leaving only the mustache. My image of sailors, at least the modern-day version, did not include a beard. I felt nervous.

At first I couldn't find Bruce. The crewmen working on the USA took time out from their chores to give me a short "What the hell are you doing here?" look as I walked toward them. I quickly glanced at each crewman, anticipating Bruce's smiling face, but he wasn't there, unless he was working below decks.

"Have you seen Bruce Epke?" I asked one of the crew. He told me to ask someone else, and as I turned away I heard him suggest to another crewman that they should post a guard at the top of the ramp so that tourists, nobodies, Lookie-Lous, geeks, hangers-on, groupies, lost walkers, and lost souls would not wander down the ramp and bother the crew.

Instead of looking for someone else to ask, I looked at the USA. The impression of simplicity that I had when standing along the railing was now gone. Close-up she was an intricate beauty, very complicated with blocks and winches and a thousand yards of lines tying it all together. The towering aluminum mast seemed grossly out of proportion, as though it had been made for a much larger boat. Not a sliver of wood except for the flagstaff on the very stern could be seen on any part of the yacht.

The sixty-foot hull shone with a fresh white glaze like a newly painted car. Slicing across the whiteness was a thin silver and red stripe about six inches below the gunnel that ended with the words "Pacific Telesis." What the hell was Telesis? It sounded like a rare tropical disease, but it turned out to be the phone company and the syndicate's major sponsor.

Three opened hatches, two in the front and one midship, led to a black undefined world below decks. I peered into the middle hatch, and one of the crewmen I hadn't noticed before, peered out. It wasn't Bruce, and I looked away. Cordless drills, wrenches, hammers were scattered over the topsides—it looked as though it had rained tools only a few minutes before. Everyone was working fast, and needless to say, I felt very out of place.

Finally someone told me Bruce was probably in the equipment trailer. This was my casual introduction to 12-meter America's Cup sailing and the crew of the USA. Along the east side of the yacht club, two hundred yards from the 12-meter dock, next to a little alcove where a few old men sat drinking rum and playing cards, I found the forty-foot container to which I had been directed. I was surprised at my first glance inside: this solid steel box with its bland industrial exterior was outfitted like a high-class marine supply store, including a workbench and shelves and every form of power tool known to man. In the back of the container I could see Bruce hot-knifing the end of a line to keep it from fraying. I walked to the back of the container and watched him work for a moment. A biting, foul odor drifted from the burning nylon line, but I doubt that Bruce even noticed the stench. He put down the knife just long enough to shake my hand.

"Hey, good to see you," he said.

"Yeah, same here."

"Listen, we launch in five minutes, so give me a hand with the sails." Bruce was a good-looking man, about six-foot-four, 220 pounds, with very little body fat—a strong, well-muscled athlete. Rowing for the University of Pennsylvania and on several national teams, including the 1980 Olympic team, had made him hard and tough and instilled in him a self-confidence that I passionately envied. He said little in the way of small talk, and I've been with him for hours when he didn't say a word.

Two or three times a day his eyes narrowed down, and he displayed a lightning-quick temper. In rowing we called these characters "heaters," and Bruce was a classic, supreme heater. Bruce heated up at least once a day, something everyone dreaded, though we knew his outbursts occurred for only one reason: more than anyone, he sought perfection in all our crew maneuvers, and he settled for nothing less. Bruce also publicly acknowledged, loud and clear and in front of everyone, a job well done. The magnitude of the job was unimportant: if you did something well, remembered a new technique, or simply kept your head in a dangerous situation, Bruce pointed it out. He complimented you in a sincere, straightforward manner that made you feel so good you couldn't wait for it to happen again.

Bruce's nickname in the yachting world was Sheik, and everyone called him Sheik Bruce or Sheik Epke or just plain Sheik. He had acquired that nickname during the summer of 1983 when he was a grinder on the America's Cup hopeful Defender. In some obscure movie every character in a little band of pirates had the title Sheik dropped in front of his regular name, so they called each other Sheik Gary or Sheik Charlie—the head of this band of pirates was named Sheik Bruce. Being a natural leader and possessing sheik-like nobility, Bruce was given this nickname with universal acceptance. He had now moved up a notch on the ladder of crew success to the rank of sewerman on the USA. "I'm in charge of everything that goes on below decks," he told me, "in the sewer."

Bruce's love—his passion—was classical music. We would sit in the Sheik-van in a distant corner of the St. Francis parking lot and listen to Gustav Mahler's First Symphony, the Titan. I could see the windsurfers ripping the water in front of Crissy Field, but Sheik had his eyes closed—better to hear the music. Mahler was talking to him now, real intensely and only to him. Bruce had the music turned up so stinking loud, his face all contorted as the good part drew near. He reveled in the music like no one I've ever seen. And if it wasn't enough, he rewound the tape and played the good part again: "Now listen," he said every time. "Listen to the horns—hear it? Listen again— this is it, now listen. Hear it? Hear those horns?" He would roll in his seat a few seconds and pull his knees up to his chest—completely mad with happiness.

We walked to the sail loft, and Bruce pointed to a 1.5-ounce spinnaker stuffed into a giant nylon laundry bag, known as a turtle. He grabbed a similar sail as we returned to the USA where only five minutes before I had been given the standard cold shoulder. This time I was with Bruce, one of their own, and that made all the difference in the world. Bruce introduced me to a few of the crewmen—Russ, Tommy, Jim Plagenhoef, alias *Flog the Winch* because of his skill at repairing the many winches. The big man, Skipper Thomas D. Blackaller, Jr., had not arrived.

"Just one thing to remember," Bruce said. "Stay on the boat. What I mean is, don't fall overboard."

"Yeah, thanks, good advice." That shouldn't be a problem, I thought, except for some reason the railings around the edge of the deck had been left off the master plan. A missed step or sudden shifting in the boat, and it would be 'Adios, hope you can swim.' Tumbling overboard was the last thing I wanted to do this afternoon. The water looked sickly brown from the flood runoff. It was ice cold in the San Francisco bay tradition and definitely not for swimming, only drowning.

But I wasn't worried about drowning right then. More important, I wanted to be put in a situation where the possibility of drowning existed: I wanted to go sailing. My presence as beginner-grinder was now known, but no word had yet been given as to whether I would sail or watch from the tender or wave from the dock. The best thing, I figured, was to stay on board until ordered elsewhere.

I went below decks and helped Bruce with the sail preparations. All the sails, a dozen jibs and spinnakers, had to be arranged carefully so that they could be hoisted with a minimum of delay. My first look at the sewer caught me off guard: other than the cold metal ribs and plywood floorboards, it was completely barren. No kitchen, head, or bunks cluttered this basement. Some extra lines hung from a wire, and other than the sails the sewer was as empty as a moving van.

"Grab on to the spinnaker when I tell you," Bruce said, "and squeeze it together while I tie a loop of yarn around it." I sat on the plywood floorboards and tried to figure out what we were doing. About every yard he would tell me to squeeze while he tied. Gradually we turned the huge billowing spinnaker into a trussed-up, three-headed snake. The idea, Bruce explained, was to keep the spinnaker from unfurling in a tangled mess when it was hoisted up the mast. Once hoisted, the yarn wraps, called stops, would break free, and the spinnaker would fill like a butterfly spreading its wings. Although over the next year I saw it countless times, I never tired of seeing a spinnaker burst open and come to life.

"By the way," he asked in an offhanded tone, "do you know how to sail?"

"Sure," I told him. "I won an awesome coffee cup for finishing third in C-class at the 1973 Ancient Mariner Hobie Cat regatta."

He didn't seem impressed. I explained to him that I had a feel for the mechanics of sailing, how the boat goes upwind in a zigzag manner and the difference between tacking and jibing. I thought about my whole sailing experience for a few moments and then concluded to him that, overall, I didn't know any proper sailing terms for various maneuvers or even the correct names for the myriad puzzle pieces that make up a 12-meter. I just had a basic feel for sailing.

I soon learned that one of the worst aspects of joining this team was that I had to re-learn the all-important port and starboard. In the rowing world of my last decade I had faced backward, so port was on my right side. Now that I was looking straight ahead, port and starboard (left and right) were reversed.

"Now listen," Bruce said as we worked, "you'll learn the terms fast enough. The important thing here is to keep everybody straight: the main guy here is Tom Blackaller. If you get on his bad side, you're gone. And then there's Kenny Keefe. He actually runs this show, like the general manager. And J.T. He's in charge of money. And Hank, well, Hank is in tight with all these guys, so you have to toe the line with him also."

By the time we left the dock I had about thirteen "just one thing to remember" rules on my mind.

18

2
Blacky

As we finished with the spinnaker a deep throaty rumble began vibrating the aluminum cage where Bruce and I worked. This noise came from the tender, Trojan Lady, moving alongside the USA.

The tender is used for towing the 12-meter to and from open sailing ground since a 12-meter is not equipped with its own engine. The USA syndicate had acquired the use of an especially nice tender, a forty-five-foot, ultra-plush combination powerboat and bordello.

"The tender is on loan from Trojan Yachts," Bruce told me. "You've heard of Trojan Yachts, haven't you? From Lancaster, Pennsylvania?"

I didn't know any brand names, but I had a deep dislike for the concept. I had battled these bilious powerboats every day of my rowing career. They had wreaked havoc on an infinite number of calm Sunday mornings, turning the placid water inside out. I was glad to finally have a constructive use for these brutes.

The captain of the Trojan Lady had now throttled back on the engines, and over the low purring I heard a shrill voice say, "What's the holdup? Good morning, Kenneth. Everybody here? Where are the lunches?"

Skipper Tom Blackaller had arrived.

Later I reflected how appropriate it had been that my first contact with Tom Blackaller was only with his voice. If I had seen him approaching, I might have been put off by his round, un-athletic figure. His voice was youthful, very energetic, audible even over the noise of the tender. If I had seen him driving up to the dock, I would have noticed his BMW sedan with the license plate DFENDER announcing his past America's Cup failure. I always thought it was strange that he would voluntarily immortalize his defeat rather than attempt, at least outwardly, to put it aside and move on to new challenges.

Blackaller had a persona that was made for the media. He could have been a very successful television personality. His speech was always decisive and never marred by an errant *you know*. Basically he had two personalities. One was the fun, storytelling Blacky where he kept us laughing with his farfetched tales about the good old days of yacht racing and the equally important after-race parties. He could tell a story.

The other Blackaller was his patented, patron-to-waiter personality. Here, Blackaller played the rich, haughty, spoiled restaurant patron while we – his crew – assumed the role of groveling waiters. Blacky's tone went far beyond a sarcastic to the Blackaller range, best exemplified by his common phrase when things were not going well: "Okay, girls, let's try not to fuck up this tack."

Eventually I wanted, if only for a minute or two, to talk with Blackaller without the bullshit. Just to talk like two quasi-normal people. Months later in Fremantle I needed a ride from the team house to the compound, and Blacky was my only recourse. As we sat together in his compact car for the three-mile ride and talked fairly steadily, he never, not for a single minute, gave me the impression that he was talking to me as if I were anything other than a slave, a novice sailor, a potential sponsor, a mirror, or as though I were not even there.

Nonetheless I preferred Blackaller to almost any other America's Cup skipper. At least he kept things interesting, like the time he found out his favorite porno star, Traci Lords, was only fifteen years old when she made her first porn movies. "I am so stinking happy," Blacky said, dancing with excitement. "I've got a dozen Traci Lords movies at home. Oh, man, you should see her in this bathtub with this other girl. The tub's filled with paint or mud or something, and they're going at it like two wildcats."

I often heard less than complimentary remarks made in our skipper's direction, but I knew from experience that every successful man has his detractors. At least Blacky wasn't afraid to flaunt his quirks in public. Hell he wore them like a general wears his medals.

When Bruce and I finished with the last spinnaker, he suggested the time was right for me to meet the big man. I climbed through the hatch just as Blackaller announced he wanted to go from our current side-tow to a bow-tow.

"Cast off lines," Blacky yelled.

Unfortunately someone neglected to release the stern line at the right moment, and now the USA was veering straight for the concrete seawall at eight knots an hour. Blackaller madly turned the wheel, trying to get us back on course, the whole time spending $100 curses like it was payday. The USA was slow to respond and a collision seemed imminent. About ten feet from impact the slack pulled out of the bow line, and we straightened back on course. Wow, that was close.

A second later Bruce grabbed my arm and introduced me to Blacky.

"Are you the Stockton Stud?" he wanted to know.

"The what?" I asked, utterly confused.

"No," Bruce said, "he's the Rowing Flash, our guest grinder."

3
The Big Grind

I turned from Blackaller and walked to the starboard grinder handles. For this first outing I had been assigned to grind under the watchful eye of the starboard trimmer, Hank Stuart, a difficult instructor who consistently found fault with everyone. I didn't care—I was just glad to be there.

While we towed to the sailing zone I sized up the handles, giving them a good visual going-over before I engaged in any funny stuff. The handles shone like bright jewelry, reflecting the whole world in their chrome. The black anodized grinding pedestal supported the handles in the middle, and on the front side of the pedestal a huge pair of wire cutters had been attached with duct tape. "This is in case of emergencies," Bruce told me. For instance, if the jib sheet wraps around a grinder's leg, the wire or the leg might need a quick trim.

Two full-time grinders, a port and starboard grinder, were needed to keep the 12-meter plowing along, with each grinder taking instructions from his respective trimmer. The handles were designed so that in a big wind two more crewmen, usually Sheik and the bowman, could jump in on the opposite side of the full-time grinders. On this first day I nodded to my counterpart, Tommy Ducharme, who would operate the port handles. He looked a little concerned that I didn't know what I was doing.

I stepped forward, bent slightly at the waist, spread my legs a few inches wider than shoulder width, and placed a hand on each of the two grips.

"Head up," Hank said. "You have to watch the foredeck at all times." I quickly lifted my downward gaze. For my whole rowing career coaches had been telling me to keep my head up. How refreshing, I thought, to know that some things never change. I couldn't help smiling.

I spun the handles a few tentative turns. The primary winch just to my right responded with a few low clicks. So far, so good. Of course the sails hadn't been hoisted, so naturally the jib sheet wasn't attached to the winch—that reduced the resistance to nothing. I reversed direction and spun again—fewer clicks came out of the winch, corresponding to the lower gear. My apprenticeship concluded at that moment with Blackaller's piercing call: "Hoist main."

The mainsail halyard (the line used for hoisting the sail) was led to the starboard primary winch, and on Hank's command port grinder Tommy Ducharme and I, along with sewerman Bruce and bowman Scott Inveen, began turning the handles in the heaviest gear. The huge mainsail slowly crept up the mast. With the mainsail three-quarters of the way up the mast we reversed directions and finished in second gear.

A minute later Bruce and Scott Inveen hoisted by hand, or *bounced*, the jibsail to its top mark. This front sail is smaller than the mainsail and much lighter, and therefore two strong men pulling on the halyard, hand over hand, can get it into position. With the sails up and plenty of wind, my grinding audition was ready to begin.

Grinding. The word itself serves as an accurate jib description. Grinding sounds simple, and the actual grinding motion is very simple. If you feel like giving it a try, turn your bicycle upside down and spin the pedals with your hands. Now, to get a real feel for grinding, have someone put on the brakes until it is almost impossible to move the pedals. Then instruct your favorite enemy to stick a garden hose in your face and turn it on full blast. Now tilt the whole thing on its side and have someone with a full sailing vocabulary like Tom Blackaller yell at you to turn faster. This is the essence of grinding.

I had to learn a few other details: the proper way to change gears and the proper way to switch between the port and starboard winch, so that the two grinders can be linked together or work independently. But no one expected me to learn these intricacies on the first day. They wanted to see me grind, and they wanted to see me grind fast.

"Speed is the only thing that's important," Bruce warned.

He explained that the faster the sail can be brought in snug to the rail, the less time it will take for the boat to get up to speed. A tacking duel might take twenty or more tacks, and if we could cinch up the jib two seconds faster than the grinders on the opposing boat, then we could change the outcome of a race.

We practiced for two hours, tacking, jibing, spinnaker sets, rounding the marks, and suddenly it was race time. In rowing, I might have spent seven or eight months training in my single scull before I raced any opponent more challenging than my stopwatch. But this was yacht racing, a whole new world that knew absolutely no competitive restraint. Our crew had been prodded by the sight of Heart of America bearing down on us, and we didn't hesitate to put our reputations on the line. My first sail quickly became a learn-as-you-go scrimmage, and I did my best to decipher the rapid orders that came from every direction.

Our opponent, the Chicago syndicate's Heart of America, was affectionately nicknamed "The Old Blue Stove." She was a veteran of America's Cup competition and was now about a hundred yards astern, with the spinnaker set and a full head of steam. We hoisted our newest spinnaker, a North Sails beauty, $15,000 plus tax, fragile as an eggshell, affectionately called *the billboard* because of its *Pacific Telesis* logo. We turned on a parallel course, and the Heart caught up to us in a blink. The battle was joined.

We stayed ahead of Heart of America for about five minutes, lumbering past Alcatraz, sliding in front of the Sausalito ferry with a hundred businessmen in button-down shirts crowding the rail and wishing they could be in our place. Then the Heart started to creep past. A minute later they were three lengths in front, and the excuses started bouncing around our boat: "The current is more favorable where they are; wind is weaker here; tides are funny; we aren't using the right spinnaker; he's pointing lower, higher, different," and finally "What's he doing?" He was going faster than we were, plain and simple, and faster is faster in any sport.

"We'll catch him on the upwind leg," Bruce said.

Fifteen seconds after Heart of America spun around the mark and headed for the finish line Blackaller yelled, "Drop the spinnaker." The spinnaker collapsed through the forward starboard hatch with Bruce on the tugging end, cursing like a Blackaller protégé. The jib was pulled tight, and we started into a tacking duel in twenty-five knots of true wind. I dug my feet into the deck—this was more like it. I hadn't driven four hundred miles for nothing—I was loving every wild second.

Bruce slipped into the grinder spot directly in front of me, and Scott Inveen stood next to him. The handles flew fast and furious now that all four grinder spots were manned, and on one tack I lost my grip. I might have stepped back and taken a picture because the handles were a blur of spinning motion. I could not reclaim my grip until the tack was completed, at least not without risking a broken finger. After being *spun off the handles*, the ultimate in grinder humiliation, I kept my hands glued to the grips.

Blackaller stayed on each tack for about thirty seconds, giving the grinders just enough time to close-haul the jib, take a deep breath, and then start the process over again. The cockpit was alive with frantic yelling—encouragement, instructions, curses. Everyone had something to say except the grinders. Someone shouted that we were catching them, but I couldn't tell. "Helms alee," was all I listened for, the words meant it was tacking time again.

A fantastic rhythm began to emerge after ten or twelve tacks as everyone worked at maximum effort. The sail trimmers released the jib at the right moment, and the grinders spun the handles with every ounce of strength. I thought we were gaining.

The buoy in front of the St. Francis Yacht Club marked the finish line, about half a mile to go, and we still trailed the Heart by two lengths. But we had another problem: the Golden Bear tour boat was charging down at full speed in a big hurry to reach Pier 33 for another load of passengers. The Golden Bear was not going to change course for a couple of day sailors like us. Blackaller tacked first to keep clear of the Golden Bear, and we assumed Buddy Melges, skippering Heart of America, would do the same. Perhaps Buddy didn't see the Bear, or maybe he had something else on his mind, but regardless of the reason, he held his course. It appeared from our slowly sinking vantage point that the Heart's bow cleared the poop deck of the Bear with just enough room to fit in a short curse. The victory went to the Old Blue Stove.

Back on the dock, Buddy Melges told both crews a very funny joke about Mike Ditka, William 'the Refrigerator' Perry, and a snapping turtle. Every crewman stood on his boat or on the dock, listening to Buddy, the classic, unhurried showman. I watched Blackaller as Buddy told his joke. Blacky looked envious, as though he were trying to think of his own joke to tell the crews, but he never spoke. Buddy won the battle on the dock, as well as on the water.

I helped wash the boat, the whole time hoping that someone of authority would take me aside and tell me if I'd passed the first test. I liked the sailing and the crewmen, and I wanted to be invited back. Certainly someone would say, "You did okay. See you tomorrow." That never happened. Basically, I was not told, "Don't come back." I soon learned that on this team a lack of disapproval could be considered acknowledgment for a job well done. Bruce told me the team had a morning workout and I was welcome. As far as the sailing went, he couldn't say if I would be needed. "Be patient," he said. "You'll know soon enough."

4
The St. Francis Yacht Club

My second day on the job I followed Bruce's instructions and reported to the fancy San Francisco Bay Club for the team's workout. As I drove from my temporary home, a friend's house in the Sunset District, I became lost on the way and arrived a few minutes late. Habitual tardiness has cursed my whole life.

But this being Saturday, one of the holy days of sleeping late, the Bay Club's doors remained locked. I waited thirty minutes with another crewman, and finally pronounced our effort a lost cause. The other USA sailors had never bothered to show up for fear of missing breakfast at the St. Francis Yacht Club. As in rowing, in sailing food is the first priority.

I drove to the St. Francis, put on my running clothes, and ran to the Golden Gate Bridge. When I reached the parking lot underneath the South Tower, I stopped for a few minutes and watched a dozen surfers waiting for a wave in the shadow of the bridge. Along with my computer and a box of books, I had brought my surfboard from Newport. Now I couldn't wait to surf the powerful northern California waves when I had a few hours to myself.

I discovered almost immediately, however, that by joining Camp 12-meter I had surrendered that one commodity I valued more than any other—time to myself. I never surfed while in San Francisco, or read any books, or wrote more than a handful of letters. Whatever free minutes I had in the evening I spent making notes about our sailing on my computer. Never in my life had my time been so completely occupied by one single interest.

This Saturday morning, only my second day in San Francisco, my life assumed a rhythm that defined my days until the America's Cup concluded: early morning workout, breakfast at the yacht club, mid-morning work on the boat, afternoon sailing or more work, and finally dinner at the yacht club. We worked six or seven days a week—all day with no breaks except for lunch. My alarm snapped me to attention at 5:15 a.m., and I usually returned home about 8:30 or 9:00 p.m.

There is no better place to sail 12-meters than San Francisco, especially out of the St. Francis Yacht Club. Inside the St. Francis a fantastic trophy case in the main hallway always caught my attention. Yachting has elevated the token prize concept to a terrific level—one trophy, no larger than a table lamp, showed a race being held in gale-force seas with yachts scattered to the four corners and others running into each other. The race committee boat is sinking, and a pod of killer whales devour the survivors; a brace of mermaids are swimming in formation to the crew's rescue while a man with a shotgun stands on the sinking boat's deck about to fire off a round to acknowledge the winner of the race. The winning skipper looks remarkably like Gregory Peck's Captain Ahab. The devil appears to have second place wrapped up.

A 1984 silver Olympic medal, won by John Bertrand in the Finn, held a dubious place of honor in the trophy case. Whenever our port trimmer, Russell Silvestri, walked past he remarked, "That should be my medal, and it should be gold." Eventually I came to know the reason for Russ's fury as though it were my own.

I watched the junior sailing program, windsurfing lessons, dingy races, fancy-dress celebrations, brunches, lunches, happy hours, and formal dinners, and I came to one conclusion: the heart of St. Francis pumped contentedly in the bars. Two bars catered to their drinking pleasure: the open bar for sociable men and women, and the men-only bar.

The men-only bar provided a cozy haven for the many regulars who lined the bar every night of the week except Monday. They played dominoes, or watched the fog wrap around the Marin headlands, or sat in front of the big-screen television while they drank. The same faces sat at their familiar places within the bar, drinking Mt. Gay Rum and eating toasted goldfish crackers out of wicker baskets. The regulars called themselves *The Boys at the Bar.*

The core of our fund-raising team belonged to that club, and one afternoon we took The Boys sailing. They really enjoyed themselves, taking a turn at the wheel and attempting a few clicks at the grinder handles. Unfortunately, when we docked, one Boy fell through the starboard hatch—he left by ambulance. He survived with only a small scar and a wicked headache to show for his plunge.

The club fed us extremely well in a private dining room with our favorite Filipino waiters, Manny and Miguel, slipping us Lowenbrau after Lowenbrau even after our bar privileges had been summarily cut off. The waiters, cooks, and dishwashers had an amazingly cool attitude. Overall, the members tolerated our intrusion with phenomenal patience. At least once a week we escorted some curious member—invariably a club officer—off our dock without bothering to explain the safety factors or insurance reasons. I hope a few toasts rattled the bar's window when we pulled up stakes and headed down under.

That was to occur months in the future—I had yet to sail a second time.

5
Second sail

Hurray! Sweet news. While Bruce and I worked below decks on spinnaker wrapping, Kenny Keefe stuck his head through the hatch and told me that I was sailing again today, as starboard grinder. Yesterday was fantastic—today could only be better. A moment later Kenny told me the other grinder was to be George Horvat, an ex-rower like me, who had actually been my first double scull partner ten years before.

We safely cleared the seawall without any of yesterday's fireworks, and immediately Blackaller asked if any sandwiches were on board. The call for sandwiches echoed from stem to stern, and within a blink a box of sandwiches plopped at his feet. Skipper Blacky chose first, and for a moment I wondered why: was it because he had asked, because he was the oldest, or because he was the skipper? He selected a cream cheese, cranberry, and sliced turkey sandwich that weighed at least two pounds and passed the box along. I hoped his heart was up for the challenge. By the time the box came my way only one lonely salami sandwich was left.

As I ate I noticed the guy sitting across from me was looking in my direction with great concentration. I didn't recognize him from yesterday. In fact, I'd never seen him before in my life. Wait a minute—it was George Horvat, only much bigger. He had recognized me, and now we shook hands. George made the boat after all.

We settled onto the smooth bay and immediately hoisted the main and jibsails—then we waited for the wind. All the local knowledge on board agreed the wind would be along in a minute. We waited for ten minutes, twenty minutes, but without the muddy brown tide carrying us toward the Golden Gate Bridge we would have been dead in the water. To speed up the process Blackaller called for the tender, and a minute later we were under tow for the wide-open world beyond the Golden Gate.

Again we cast off and pretended to sail but mainly we rolled in the long deep swells. I regretted having eaten that salami sandwich an hour before. The swells had a bit of muscle behind them, nice three- to four-footers in close intervals. If any surfers were still under the bridge, they had some decent waves on the way. The wind was a different matter. On Hank's order, George and I climbed onto the railing and held the boom away from the cockpit to keep it from rattling around the middle of the boat. We looked like two guys pushing a car that had run out of gas. A hundred yards away we could see two crewmen on the Heart of America in a similar pose.

33

Finally Blackaller called for the tender and we towed home, leaving the Heart to flounder in the waves. As a gesture of goodwill, our tender went after the Heart after our USA was safely tied to the dock. The Chicago team was still looking for its own tender, but the price had to be right—free usage. Until now they had managed to sail their boat right up to the dock, which was a source of tremendous pride among the Chicago team. We might have been able to do that trick, but with our tender close at hand we never tried.

A corny little poster in my old rowing boathouse claimed, "If there is no wind, row." 12-meter sailing was slightly different: if there is no wind, work on the boat. That was exactly what we did—checking the rig, shortening the lines, moving winches to more efficient locations. This was only the fifth time our craft had left the dock, so a few thousand changes were due.

I embarked on what was to become my specialty—cleaning the boat.

Lacking any professional skills such as mastery of hydraulics or electronics, I inevitably caddied for one of the veterans or cleaned the boat. I didn't like the work or being ordered about, but I did it, day after day, without complaining. Eventually I specialized in cleaning the bilge.

Bilge cleaning is an art, although like many artists my work was seldom appreciated. Part one was to remove the floorboards in sections with a cordless drill. Part two was to vacuum all of life and sailing's detritus with a wet/dry shop vacuum. The noise of a shop vacuum in that enclosed cave was like fine tuning a jet engine at full rpm. The lighting was always bad, and the inspectors wanted the bilge to be pristine. The ultimate check was to run your hand along the aluminum plating and feel for debris.

Besides the noise and cramped workspace, the main source of bilge-cleaning amusement were "meathooks"—needle-sharp little aluminum shavings, the remnants from drilling thousands of holes in the body of our 12-meter. The meathooks lodged in your fingers and stabbed your hands. They make you scream like a baby and curse your life. Your whole body shook while you pulled them out, trying not to break off the tip. Meathook wounds took a long time to heal.

George Horvat never returned to our little fraternity, mainly because he worked a normal job like most normal people.

On the following day we led a boat parade around the bay, which had been created by our syndicate's promotional team to generate some interest in the USA. The day after the parade we towed the boat to Sausalito, to Anderson's Boat Yard to be specific, and embarked on a slightly less glamorous side of the America's Cup. Anderson's Boat Yard was where the real work started.

6
Anderson's Boat Yard

"See any white lines painted on the ground?"
"No."
"Then this ain't no fucking parking lot, is it?"
"I guess not."
"Then I suggest you move your fucking car before I pick it up with the Travelift and drop it off the dock."

The man who spoke the long lines in this classic verbal exchange was Ron Anderson, owner and operator of Anderson's Boat Yard in Sausalito. Our crewman Russ Silvestri spoke the short lines. All observers agreed that if Russ had said one more word, Ron would have stuffed him into the glove compartment of his Dodge Colt and submitted the whole thing to an impromptu float test.

On my fourth day in San Francisco I was introduced to Ron Anderson and his little Sausalito kingdom. Over the next six months I spent more time at Anderson's than at the St. Francis Yacht Club. This grimy little boat yard was a four-mile tow across the harbor from the St. Francis, and some of my favorite times of the whole campaign occurred during the 1:00 a.m. towing sessions when we dragged our boat back home. I loved being awake and working at that late hour, bundled in foul-weather gear yet still freezing, the fog horn bellowing clear and cool, and invariably wagering with Russell and Craig Healy as to the time we'd step onto the St. Francis dock. The tide defined the towing times since our 12-meter drew quite a bit of water. At low tide we could not use Anderson's lifting dock without running aground. For some reason high tide always occurred around 1:00 a.m.

During our first visit to Anderson's Boat Yard, Kenny decided we needed more privacy, and a few days later the huge shed where we worked was fitted with two 1,000 lb. doors that required three or four men to open and close.

That shed became our clubhouse. Be at Anderson's tomorrow morning. We're having a fairing party at Anderson's. Get your ass over to Anderson's and clean up the mess. Anderson's meant work.

Ron Anderson was a classic boat-yard owner. He was our dry-dock landlord, our security guard, our mocking onlooker. He hated us with a fine passion. He thought we were lazy. Everyone was lazy compared to him. Ron was short and thick, and you could no more fight him than you could fight a rhinoceros. He wore his plaid flannel shirt like armor plating. Ron strode around the yard on his ruined knees, whether to the lunch truck or to check on a customer's boat or to his private toilet with the same doggedness as the Terminator.

He had been on the 1980 Olympic sailing team, crewing for Bill Buchann in the Star. Had it not been for Carter's ridiculous Olympic boycott they probably would have won. I'm fairly certain an Olympic gold medal would have improved Ron's disposition, if only marginally

Ron had the most profitable boat yard on the West Coast, and seeing him drive up on a Sunday morning in his aqua-green Ferrari 308 GTS helped emphasize the point. The yachts flew in and out of Anderson's. Some stayed a day or two, a week for a complete overhaul, and each boat represented a few thousand dollars in gross income. Ron had a crew of surly Portuguese that worked at a fast pace all day, until they saw Ron approaching, and then they sprinted. I heard a rumor that Ron knew the immigration service phone number by heart.

Ron's main tool was an enormous four-legged beast called a Travelift. He would drive it to the end of a U-shaped dock and lower two big slings into the water. Then his assistant would position the slings underneath a waiting boat. If you were standing behind the Travelift at that moment, the damp exhaust from the diesel engine would slick back your hair as Ron stomped on the gas pedal, lifting the boat out of the water with amazing ease.

Ron drove his Travelift with the same speed and predictability as a bronco careening around a rodeo. He taught his Portuguese workers to drive the same way, and I figured everyone drove those huge beasts in a frenzied manner—until we arrived in Fremantle. The Travelift world moved in slow motion down under: no more racing around the yard. This, I've since discovered, was the usual speed for motoring a Travelift around a boat yard. Word from Anderson's reached us in Fremantle around Christmastime that made me think of Ron's frantic driving—a boat owner had fallen in front of the Travelift, and one of his legs had been crushed and was later amputated. A Portuguese had been driving, and I expected lawsuits, police investigations, and Geraldo Rivera busting the case wide open. The accident was never mentioned in the papers.

Only two men on our team were tight with Ron: Kenny Keefe, who had worked for eight years as Ron's yard manager, and Stevie Ericson. All three looked like brothers, carrying most of their ballast low and in thick chunks, and all were successful Star crewmen. Kenny Keefe was Ron's disciple, using Ron's labor-intensive approach to every task. When added together we must have spent close to a million hours in that cursed shed, always working, hoping to get the job done so we could go sailing.

Stevie was the unanimous choice by Ron, Kenny, and the rest of the crew for spearheading today's project. Our boat, USA, E-1, was not a true 12-meter. It weighed just a few thousand pounds too much, and the easiest way to cure that ailment was to remove some weight from the solid lead keel.

As Stevie revved up his newly issued Black and Decker fourteen-inch chain saw, Kenny drew a rough square on the keel in orange crayon. The keel looked about a foot thick where Kenny had marked it, and we all stood back while Stevie tentatively eased the madly spinning chain to the lead. When chain saw meets lead, funny things start to happen: the lead chips fly away like slow-speed bullets. A fragrant blue cloud of exhaust enveloped Stevie and most of the shed. The noise created by that union jarred a simple thought around your brain until it disintegrated. As in every task, Stevie dove into the keel giggling with enthusiasm. Six hours later Stevie was still hacking away at the brittle mess.

We stayed only a week on this first visit, but it seemed like more. This ratio of sailing to boat work stayed consistent throughout the challenge: roughly three days of work for every day of sailing. I kept hoping it would change, forever believing that eventually we would sail every day, but that never happened. Only our favorite pastime of watching Ron Anderson scurry around his boat yard helped alleviate the tedium. I felt much better about life when we quit the shed five days later and towed E-1 back to the St. Francis. The next day we were to go sailing.

7
Down the Hatch

I enjoyed lugging the spinnakers and jibs from the drying room to the boat. Carrying the sails, similar to carrying my oars to the dock before rowing, acknowledged to everyone that we were finally going to do what we planned, worked for, thought about, and talked about. We were going sailing.

An America's Cup 12-meter yacht is allowed a crew of eleven men, no more, which is simply not enough to do it right, at least not in a big wind. Any other sixty-six-foot ocean racer would carry a crew of twenty. Our crew of eleven was divided into three groups: afterguard, midship crew, and fore-deck.

The afterguard consisted of the skipper, tactician, and navigator—they made the big decisions, and naturally they made the big money. Our skipper was Tom Blackaller. Craig Healy was the navigator, or "naviguesser" as we usually called him. Paul Cayard, who had yet to join our team, was to be our tactician.

The midship crewmen are the two jib trimmers (also called tailors), the two grinders, and the main sheet trimmer. On our beast Hank Stuart was the starboard trimmer. Russ Silvestri was the port trimmer. Stevie Ericson trimmed the main. Stevie, a 1984 Olympic gold medalist in the Star, remembered me from the whirlwind tour of the country to which all Olympic medalists were treated. Actually, he mostly remembered my girlfriend, a remarkably beautiful woman who had accompanied me on the trip. Stevie and I talked often about the Olympics and the tour. That had been a great time for both of us.

The foredeck consists of the sewerman, bowman, and pitman, who usually work as a separate unit within the crew. The pitman is the quarterback. He sits in a scooped-out hole directly to the stern of the mast. He's surrounded by half a dozen winches that control the raising and lowering of the jib and spinnaker. All three foredeck men work in tight unison. They have to be extremely agile to work on the pitching foredeck without falling overboard. They must also be strong enough to lift the sails out of the sewer. More than anything, the foredeck crew hate surprises from the afterguard, such as a late call to hoist a different jib as the boat approaches the leeward mark.

April 1, for only the second time, we sailed beneath the Golden Gate Bridge. But unlike the previous outing, today the water was angry. The Canadian 12-meter, Canada II, was near us. In fact, we were racing, and I think we were losing. I was never sure where we were during a race, either relative to the other boat or in relation to the real world. I still had a tendency to keep my head down.

On this blustery afternoon we had just rounded the windward mark and were heading downwind. The Pacific Telesis spinnaker was perfectly filled, and the mainsail was fully extended. Everything was fine except the jib. It had been released too soon, and bowman Tommy Ducharme had not been able to control the massive sail as it fell toward the deck. A few yards of jib had sneaked into the water, then more followed until the whole sail was overboard. Our boat ground to a screeching halt with the jib acting like a sea anchor over the starboard side.

On windward mark roundings, my job as grinder was to hustle to the foredeck and help bring the now un-needed jib under control. This was exactly one of those instances. But I was having some difficulties of my own back in the grinder pit, and my usual hasty exit from the handles to the fore-deck was delayed by about twenty seconds. That was bad.

By the time I arrived, Tommy had blown the headstay— now we had a chance to drag the jib back on deck. I grabbed the sail near the clew and leaned toward the windward side. (I found out later this was wrong: I should have been closer to the middle of the sail, in order to empty the water from the sea anchor instead of fighting against it.) The jib was incredibly heavy, weighted down by a thousand gallons of clean salt water. My feeble tugs did not make much of an impression. Naturally, I leaned harder.

I cinched my hands on the sail, and with all my weight and strength I leaned backward. The sail eased a foot. I took a step backward.

In that one step I fell through the hatch.

A clean fall. Right through. Barely bumped my forearm on the way down. Straight for the bottom. What waited for me? Two sharp-cornered aluminum lengths of pipe used as steps waited to destroy my knees. The edges of the slanted floorboards would soon be painted with my blood. The fall took a long time—long enough for me to wonder what my crewmates would think when they peeled me off the floor. Mainly I prepared myself to hurt.

My right knee struck first, not against the floorboards or steps, but against a soft nylon sailbag. Then the rest of my body curled into the bag like a cat crawling into the corner of a sofa. It appeared from every angle that I had fallen straight to the basement, the whole six feet, but really I was no more than six inches below the level of the hatch. The huge bag had held the spinnaker until seconds before, and sewerman Bruce had not taken it down because of the commotion with the jib. I had seen Bruce hang the spinnaker bag on a few occasions—four short hooks were welded to the boat's frame on either side of the hatch, and four well-placed straps on the sailbag met nicely with these hooks. To my relief, the attached bag filled the whole hatch.

I needed five full seconds to take stock of my situation—to actually believe that I had survived a fall through the hatch without a scratch. When I climbed out of the hole and resumed my quest for the overboard jib, I saw ten open-mouthed faces looking at me, waiting for a spout of blood or a curse or something to show for my downward tumble. I just nodded and went back to hauling in the jib.

Already I had learned a fair amount about grinding, thanks to Russ Silvestri. We talked every day about grinding when the boat was in Anderson's. Now I just had to learn how to sail so that I could anticipate the maneuvers. The worst sensation I had experienced so far was not knowing what to do in an emergency, such as today's jib overboard. We seemed to have our share of excitement. If we could just practice a few days without racing, then perhaps I could learn what I needed to know and not feel so useless when something went wrong.

8
Ocean Madness

In the ocean there is madness. First and foremost, there were no handrails around the outskirts of our yacht. I'm not sure if handrails would help, because the boat pitches, rolls, and bounces so much that on a rough day I could go over the handrails as easily as stepping off a curb. Without handrails the possibility of going overboard was as real as stepping on a crack when walking down the sidewalk. In other words, it's scary.

One missed step and the hardness of the deck would be replaced by the icy softness of the water. Cold on top of cold would envelop you, and then nothing more would cross your consciousness as you sank toward the bottom with 150 lbs. of sodden foul-weather gear acting as an anchor and hastening your downward trip to sleep with the fish.

Or you might stay on board and get killed by the jib sheets. The jib was controlled by two long lengths of wire, mistakenly named jib sheets, which cut through the air like angry knives. On windy days it seemed as though every tack was a gamble. I gained some strange pleasure by watching the wire as it cleared the mast and shrouds and then aimed directly for my head. The wire hissed through the air, a long sleek snake that twisted imperceptibly as though aiming for some special part of my head or neck or face. For one brief instant the wire would be so close I could taste the metal. Then it would jerk away and be coiled around the winch, except on those few occasions when the wire found its mark.

The bad accidents always occurred in a strong wind and usually when we were racing. Starboard trimmer, Hank Stuart, nearly lost an eye when slashed by the wire, and Scott Easom nearly had his head torn off his neck. Before we went sailing again I vowed to buy a helmet and eye protectors.

Occasionally I wondered why I was there. The sailing was fantastic, exciting, an unbelievable thrill. I reveled in the on-the-water challenge: grinding strong and well, learning all the maneuvers, and even memorizing the names of each piece of equipment. The work was boring, but at least it was boring for everyone. For the time being I could handle it. Perhaps the best part of this whole adventure was that I was a real, honest, functioning part of a team—team player Brad—promoter of team spirit, positive thinker, smiling cog in the team machine. I know a lot of people from my rowing days who might find that hard to believe, but it was true.

Much to my relief, I hadn't seen too many prospective grinders walking down the gangway to audition for a place on the team. For a while I was worried that some big professional football players might find their way on board, but as the weeks progressed I felt more confident that I'd be working until the last sail was folded. In keeping with the unstated team motto—no news is good news—I had never been told that I was definitely on the team. I liked the sailing and they never told me that my grinding services were no longer needed—so I stayed.

I could spin the handles fast to keep Russell satisfied, and I was sure-footed to survive those quick trips to the foredeck. I liked to make the jib go in quickly, and until they told me to leave, I'd stick around.

9
A Sunday Sail

During the last few days of ocean sailing I'd discovered a significant fact: the ocean is white. For some reason I had thought the ocean was blue, but now I knew it was white—hot white like in a laundry detergent commercial, white on white with a dash of white added for contrast. I think white when I think of the ocean.

On April 13 we had a crazy outing—the boat plunged down the face of a big swell as I balanced on the foredeck trying to keep a jibsail on board. Suddenly a six-foot wave crested over the bow and drove on me as though it had a personal grudge—then I saw white. Not even a hint of green or blue crept into the picture, only pure untouched, unfiltered white. The feeling of a wave crashing over me was strange. The cold was insignificant, and the force of the wave breaking over my back felt much stronger than I had expected. I held my breath and wondered if anyone was looking in my direction in case my grip should fail and another wave appear to wash me overboard before I had a chance to reclaim my handhold. The wave made a clean, fast exit like a very good thief, taking from me only a little time and warmth. It gave in return a taste for the respect that the ocean demands.

Sometimes when we sailed on the ocean I felt as though I was riding a horse over mile after mile of rolling hills. I felt the same giddy, up-down, slightly out-of-control intoxicating rhythm. We'd had it right on a few occasions: the sails trimmed perfectly, the wind steady and strong, no one speaking except for the briefest commands. Perfection under sail.

10
Lead Lads

I awoke to a perfect San Francisco spring day, clear and warm, a nice day to go for a long bike ride or walk along the Marin Headlands. This morning we saved a dollar on the Golden Gate Bridge toll by reporting to Anderson's Boat Yard.

Today's chore was to fill the gaping, self-inflicted hole in the keel with fourteen hundred pounds of lead. A few days after I arrived, Stevie had chopped this very same hole with a chain saw to lighten the boat.

Eight weeks later our design team had decided the lead needed to be reinstalled, which was like saying you needed to climb Mt. Everest again because the camera didn't have any film in it the first time. No one was looking forward to this task.

Our design team, the masterminds behind creating a fast 12-meter, consisted of Gary Mull, a well-known racing yacht designer, Phil Kaiko his assistant, and Kenny Keefe. Blacky could always be counted on to give his design opinion, along with a few other experts, such as our computer genius, Dr. Heiner Meldner. We had a small, intimate design group compared to some syndicates, and overall they did well in piecing together the complex 12-meter puzzle. At the time none of us thought very highly of the design team when they handed down these quirky remove/reinstall the lead decisions, but we had no alternative except to follow orders.

This first Golden Gate Challenge 12-meter, E-l, was meant to be an exact copy of the winning 1983 boat, Australia II. We needed to make E-l a true 12-meter, not too light or heavy, so that when our new boat—code name R-l for Revolutionary 1—was complete, we would have a benchmark against which to check R-l's speed.

In one of the rare occurrences all year, we found ourselves completely outmatched by the lead-filling task. Some of us were walking around in shorts and sandals— accidents waiting to happen. Safety shoes in this group, regardless of the task, were Docksides, socks not required.

The exact same lead that Stevie had taken such pleasure in freeing a few weeks ago was now melting in a huge fifty-gallon drum with four propane burners frantically working underneath. The propane heaters produced an intense roar that in pure sensory violation was almost equal to the heat being generated. A skinny, five-foot-long pipe extended from the drum to the hole. The hole had been shored up with stainless steel, and now all we had to do was get the 600-degree molten lead to the hole in a controlled fashion.

Unfortunately, time suddenly became a factor: the fifty-gallon drum was beginning to disintegrate from all the heat and excitement. One way or another, the lead would soon be making a dramatic exit. When the whole mess was molten like Thanksgiving gravy, we crowded around, dying to see it flow into the hole. Something vaguely reminiscent of making mud pies came to mind as Stevie stood on a platform stirring the caldron with a length of pipe. Tiny bits of wood and other impurities burned and smoked on the surface, and occasionally Stevie put down his pipe and ladled out the trash with a shovel.

As Stevie put down his shovel one last time he accidentally tripped open the drum's valve, and a stream of molten lead shot through the pipe, spewing a line of death. Everyone scattered to high ground while Stevie tried to shut off the valve without incinerating his hand. Within ten seconds of closing the valve the lead hardened inside the skinny pipe, and we never succeeded in knocking it loose. A pound or maybe two had found its way into the original target. Luckily no one was standing within range, or we'd be looking for another crew member. Kenny decided to rent a heavy-duty melting pot for the next day, so after cleaning up the clubhouse he freed us for the day.

I survived with only superficial injuries and went into Sausalito for a haircut. I asked the barber, an old grey man, for my usual extra-short haircut. As he clipped he said, "I haven't cut a head this short since '73. Nixon was in town, and two Secret Service agents came into my shop during their lunch break." That made me feel good.

Then I drove to the Fisherman's Wharf Sheraton to compete in the Great Grind-off. The Grind-off was a simple competition: Bruce and I against two Canadian grinders. The four of us would take turns spinning a grinding simulator for thirty seconds. The team with the highest total spins would be the winner. The machine happened to be owned by the Canadian syndicate, and not surprisingly the Canadians won.

We hadn't sailed much lately, so I couldn't expect to break any records. Still I was disappointed.

After dinner we had our first team meeting, or TM. This TM started out in fine form with the dismissal of all the girlfriends and wives from the dining room. Another round of beers was ordered, and we settled down to business.

As the syndicate manager, J.T., launched into a long and boring criticism of several things, including our guzzling of the yacht club's beer, I looked at my fellow teammates. We had about fifteen crewmen and five or six support people, depending on whether or not I counted Kent Massie. Kent was a thirty year-old millionaire who derived great sporting pleasure by driving the Trojan Lady. Kent was due to be replaced by Mik Beatie, skipper of the Tiburon ferry.

Essentially the same crew who sailed my first day in February were still here, a month later. Hank and Russ were firmly locked into their tailor pits, along with Stevie at his main sheet pedestal. Scott Easom was another jib trimmer who longed to be in Hank's place, but that was not likely to happen, judging from Blacky's fondness for Hank. The afterguard was unchanged with Blacky, Healy, and the soon-to-be introduced Paul Cayard. Our foredeck was not settled—Bruce was alone in the sewer, but two men, Jim Whitmore and Jim Plagenhoef, currently traded off in the pit. We also had two able bowmen, Tommy Ducharme and Scott Inveen. With the arrival of our new boat we would need two full eleven-man crews, so there would be plenty of work for everyone.

We'd added another grinder, Jeff Littfin, who took temporary leave from Hewlett-Packard where he was earning $40,000 a year, to pursue this every-sailor's dream. I had come to be impressed by how dedicated this fraternity had proved to be: they worked every day, all day long. Perhaps because of the long hours, this crew didn't have the same killer-intensity as my rowing mates, except Kenny Keefe, who was obsessed beyond belief. Most of these sailors were *lifers*, which means their whole lives were devoted to sailing. After the Cup they would move on to the next regatta.

We had an exclusive *all-star* team—only the best sailors were allowed on the USA. The strength and endurance I had acquired through rowing were the most important traits of a top grinder, thus I was exempt from having to qualify as an all-star sailor. The Canada and Chicago syndicates had taken a different approach: they found some local sailing talent and tried to teach them to sail 12-meters. That technique could be quite dangerous in the early learning stages. One Canada crewman had almost lost a leg a few weeks earlier when a spinnaker line accidentally wrapped around his leg while he was working in the sewer. The spinnaker suddenly refilled, and the crewman was literally launched out the hatch.

Skipper Blackaller was unable to make this first meeting, due to his racing at the Sebring Twelve Hours of Endurance. Race car driving and our current pastime, pouring lead, were both dangerous occupations, so I guess it equaled out. I hoped Blacky's race car driving would hone his skippering skills.

J.T. finally finished with his lecture and then introduced a new crew member: tactician Paul Cayard. Paul was easy to notice. He looked like a yachting version of Omar Sharif before Omar had taken up bridge. If a film is ever made about the USA, Cayard can play himself in the lead role.

By profession Cayard called himself a sailmaker, although I doubt if he could find the on/off switch on an industrial sewing machine. He was actually the sail loft's *factory rep*. After a new sail wardrobe was delivered from his loft, Cayard would accompany the owner in a regatta. Naturally, with Cayard aboard, the yacht usually won handily, thereby assuring the purchaser that he had made a good investment. I hoped he could do the same for us.

Cayard had parlayed his skippering ability into a good living. Among our syndicate only Cayard and Blackaller were making any money—Blacky through a hefty salary and Cayard (and Blacky also) by receiving a percentage on each sail our syndicate bought. Over the year we spent $1.5 million on sails.

Most of the standard crewmen like me received $1,000 per month. I found out later our crew was being paid extremely well in relation to other syndicates. The crew of Australia IV made only $70 a month, while the Stars and Stripes crewmen were paid $500 a month. Of course we all received room and board and enough expensive sailing clothing to open our own store.

Cayard, from that very first day, remained a bewildering mystery to me. In true afterguard fashion he sustained a curt distance from the other *jigs*, as he always called us. He made good use of his desk in the syndicate office, yet unlike Blackaller, Cayard lifted weights with the crew and was the second strongest bench presser on the team. A month before we left for Fremantle our trainer, Connie Jardine, hosted a three-mile run. Cayard stayed on my shoulder long after the pain he was experiencing from maximum exertion should have caused him to drop back. The look on his face was one of pure torture, but somehow he kept going. He was a tough, twenty-eight year-old man.

At this first meeting Cayard spoke a few minutes about the importance of getting our new boat, R-l, ready to sail when it arrived. The lowlight of the meeting was Cayard's last statement: "With a good showing we should get third or fourth among the challengers."

Adios, was my first thought. Why should we be spending countless dollars and all our waking hours for third or fourth place? I immediately knew Cayard had a serious attitude problem.

"He doesn't reach for the stars," Stevie said when I mentioned it to him later that night. Stevie, our other in-house Olympic gold medalist, had immediately picked up on Cayard's statement. We both agreed it did not bode well. "Cayard sets himself up for a third-place finish, and that's exactly what he gets," Stevie said. "The same exact thing happened at the Olympic Star Trials. Cayard and Keefe were our toughest competition—in fact, they were faster than us a lot of the time, but Cayard didn't have the right mental approach. I'm glad he didn't, or else Buchann and I wouldn't have won."

Perhaps I could improve Cayard's attitude. I attributed my rowing success to a clever, bearded sports guru named Mike Livingston, himself an Olympic silver medalist in rowing. Mike distilled the secrets of winning into three simple rules:

(1) Row like your life depends on it.

(2) Be humble.

(3) Take complete responsibility for the outcome of the race.

Before the 1984 Olympics my mind had been a jumbled odd lot of doubts and vague motivations until Mike helped arrange my thoughts. Why shouldn't the same rules apply to yacht racing?

A few days later I saw a young woman working out at our local gym, the Bay Club. She was an exceptionally beautiful, lean, blond woman, who caused involuntary stares from everyone who saw her.

"Now that is a beautiful woman," I said to Stevie.

Stevie laughed and said, "That's Cayard's wife, Eika."

Eika's father was Pelle Petterson, a champion sailor who had once skippered a Swedish challenge for the America's Cup.

Through rowing I've known many Swedes. I even trained in Falkenberg, on the west coast of Sweden, for several long, cold, wet, windy *summer* months. I had learned that Swedes were a quiet, reserved, classy, solid, stolid group of citizens. Eika followed suit with cool, (actually quite cold), muteness.

Six months later in Fremantle we had just finished a race and were cleaning the boat when Eika and the girls returned from an all-afternoon cruise up the Swan River. They had drunk about two cases of red wine, and Eika, in sailing terminology, was bent. She stumbled off the boat, she screamed, she laughed, she begged Paul to kiss her. The whole crew, mostly Paul, stood in complete shock. I had a great deal more respect for Eika after that, but Paul dropped a notch in my estimation by not responding to her demands. He just ignored her.

11
Blacky's Friend

We started our sail today with a small problem: we were missing one grinder. Based on previous experience, I knew I would have to train a guest grinder, and more likely than not I would have to lug the guest grinder around the practice course.

As we towed out of the harbor I reflected that over the last nine weeks, since I arrived in San Francisco, I'd gone from being a novice grinder to being a sailor capable of instructing a beginner in the fine art of grinding. I liked the feeling of knowing the right moves. It felt good.

Today's guest was a friend of Blackaller who had planned on taking pictures or something equally un-strenuous. He looked somewhat confused when pressed into service. The man walked up to the grinder handles as though he was ordering a drink in a bar: just here for a minute and then I'm going back to my table.

He asked me, "Ah, where's the safest place to be?"

I looked at him and said, "Back on the dock."

As we towed toward the bay I realized a very significant sailing fact: the wind was screaming. The bay danced with whitecaps, the spray smacked my dry suit, words disappeared the instant they left my mouth. The wind in numbers was never less than twenty-five knots, and it built from there. The choppy bay water was sure to get rougher when the tide reversed direction and opposed the wind. When that occurred, as inevitably happened, the result was like a sharp rasp scraping against the grain of the water. The bay waves would stand up even taller, and the monster whirlpools would spin us like a top.

As we sailed underneath the Golden Gate Bridge, thick ocean swells began tumbling into the cockpit. I tried to keep my feet out of the huge pool of water that quickly formed, but that was futile. Wave after wave emptied into the cockpit, and my feet turned icy cold and then went completely numb. We had planned to sail around Bonita Rock, about a mile beyond the Gate, but less than halfway there Blackaller suddenly yelled "Baring off," and we turned toward the bay.

"It's just too dangerous out here," I heard him say to Cayard, and he was right. If some disaster had occurred, the mast breaking for instance, we'd probably get sued by his friend.

John *Oddjob* Audley, a new grinder who had come to us from the Canadian syndicate, finally joined us, and the guest grinder went away. I had never bothered to introduce myself to the guest because I figured he had enough things to think about without having to learn my name.

When I first met Oddjob, I was somewhat reluctant to introduce myself to him as well. Oddjob was the original sailing thug. His background was wrestling, bone breaking, lugging 250 lb. mainsails from the container to the boat by himself. Oddjob was bred to be a grinder. Although Canadian born, Oddjob lived in some mystical land known as Kennebunkport, Maine, which qualified him to sail on the USA. Paul Cayard had an eye for a bargain, and as soon as the Canadians decided Oddjob was no longer needed, Paul offered him a short-term deal. With the new boat soon to arrive, we needed four strong grinders, and Oddjob was a good find.

Regardless of the conditions, he loved to dress weirdly: neon green wet suit, his face-painted with green zinc oxide to match. The end result was that he inevitably looked as though he had just landed from Mars. But who was to contradict his fashion sense? Only someone in need of a new nose.

After a few more hours we approached the last leeward mark, which meant we had to douse the chute for the final time.

"Chute down," Blacky yelled, and everything was going according to schedule until the supposedly dead spinnaker suddenly jumped out of the hatch and went running for wide-open spaces. The wind was still howling, and we all saw disaster taking perfect shape in front of us as the spinnaker sprouted wings and ascended into the heavens. It sailed beautifully without our assistance, and only our feeble curses tainted its otherwise excellent flight. The sail finally alit on the water about twenty yards to the stern and immediately sank. Two shackles were still attached, and to retrieve the sail we had to release one of the shackles and haul the sail on board using the last connected line. If that line broke, the $10,000 sail would be lost forever.

Tommy Ducharme popped open one of the two shackles, and the spinnaker sank even farther under the waves. Every crewman went to the stern of the boat (a place I never visited except when I was cleaning up), and we hauled the spinnaker on board the old-fashioned way: hand over hand, foot by foot, until the whole dripping mess was firmly locked into the sewer. I believe the sail came through unscathed, but unfortunately the same cannot be said for our collective psyches.

I love the way that spinnaker came alive for those few moments. It seemed to have wings.

12
Diet Coke

For some reason, little kids seem to have easy access to proud moments. For instance a good report card or perhaps running a good race. As I get older, these moments of intense satisfaction seem to become rarer and rarer.

I had that satisfying feeling yesterday as I showed Sheik a one-page article in *Sport* magazine that I had written. This was my big debut as a writer, and I had worked long and hard on the article. I was feeling on top of the world.

Later at breakfast Hank Stuart asked to see the article, and I lent him the magazine. A few minutes later he stood up at the breakfast table as though delivering a toast at some alumni banquet. He then proceeded to read my story in a nasty, sarcastic tone. He rolled his eyes and laughed at the parts that were not funny. He was enjoying himself, and he held everyone's attention. I had never seen him so animated, as though some perverse quirk within his otherwise dull personality had been awakened.

I contemplated the right move: sit there and take it with a smile, or perhaps stuff the magazine down his throat. Instead I got up and left the room.

All day I looked for a chance to nudge Hank over the gunnel, preferably while at least five miles off the California coast in the roiling *Potato Patch*, an exceptionally rough stretch of water near the Marin Headlands. People fall overboard all the time. In fact, Hank had fallen overboard once before. To my great disappointment, however, he never left his tailor pit.

My unexpected retribution occurred today. I dressed quickly in my dry suit, using the portable office next to the equipment trailer as a changing room. This office had two desks, a telephone, a roll of stamps, and a box with a few of yesterday's lunches. It lacked only one key item: a toilet.

I didn't have time to use the yacht club toilet, so I grabbed a seven-eighths-empty Diet Coke can and vented my discomfort until the can was nine-tenths full. I intended to throw the urine-filled can into the dumpster on my way to the boat. With one foot out the door I heard the phone ring. I answered the phone, made a quick note on the pad, and a minute later I was on board. The malignant Diet Coke can was now completely forgotten in the office as though it had never existed in my whole universe.

We sailed without distinction, and I went to the shower room immediately after the boat had been cleaned and groomed. Hank made for the office to make his daily phone calls. The pattern had long been in effect—Hank would inform the whole Hank lineage, regardless of area code, country, or local time, that he had survived another day at Camp 12-meter.

A short time later as I was leaving the shower room, I saw Hank walking quickly to the bathroom, where he ran hot water and commenced to wash his mouth with soft soap. I lingered by the door as he told Sheik that if he ever found out who had doctored that can of Diet Coke...

13
Cone of Silence

On May 3, we sailed under a cone of silence. The object of the drill was for the crew and captain to remain completely mute for about an hour while we sailed around the bay. But we didn't just sail—we rounded marks, flew the spinnaker, and performed a very difficult jib change during a tack.

For most of the crew, keeping silent was not easy after months of screaming out reams of information, some worthwhile but most of value equal to the cries of seagulls. The grinders, for the most part, never say anything regardless of the drill. Under the cone of silence a simple tack became a frightening maneuver since we didn't know if Blackaller was faking a tack or had accidentally spun out the stern or was really tacking. No one was hurt during the drill, and that made everything okay. The only crewmen who were in danger, as usual, were the grinders who work in the direct line of the flying chain saws, aka the jib sheets.

The cone of silence was not quite quiet. Our voices were missing, but the fantastic sailing noises still attacked my ears. The sounds of 12-meter sailing have their origins in the *primary winch.* The jib sheet strangles the winch, four wraps of quarter-inch steel wire. When the jibsail is full and tugging on the wire, the pressure exerted on the winch is estimated to be seven thousand pounds, but most of us would feel that is a conservative estimate on windy days.

When the jib is eased, the trimmer carefully runs his hand along the outside of the winch and releases about two or three inches of wire. The wire and winch rubbing together under such pressure creates an excruciating scream, like a thousand fingernails on a chalkboard, and usually my ear is no more than a foot from the source. The sound can last five seconds in a big ease, but usually the noise lasts one or two seconds. The first time I heard that sound I thought the winch was being torn from its base. Certainly something was broken or breaking or dying inside that huge stainless-steel cylinder.

That same winch makes excellent ratchet noises when we are spinning the handles. Click-clicking, a forest of grasshoppers mating in the moonlight. Spin faster and the clicks become a steady blur of ratchet music. Can we really be making that wonderful noise? The grinder handles fit so nicely into my palm. I am strong and healthy and ready for anything.

On a tack the bow swings into the wind. We turn the handles slowly at first until the clew clears the first set of shrouds. Then we spin faster until the sail is around the mast and drawing close to the sweet spot right next to the boat. One last burst of power to get the most out of first gear, and then we reverse direction with the handles and go into second gear. We spin again, and now the clew is very close to its final resting spot. The resistance soon becomes too much, so I stomp on the shift button to give us third gear, and we change direction one last time. The clew is home.

I instantly turn to get the tail and *flake* it next to the tailor pit. The tail, or excess jib sheet, might have looped around the flagstaff or possibly Blackaller's neck as a result of Russell's violent pulling.

Flaking returns the jib sheet to a neat pile next to the tailor pit. Bruce patiently taught me the proper technique for flaking: run the jib sheet through my hands, taking out the kinks and at the same time piling the sheet on the deck, as opposed to coiling the line, which gets tangled in a blink. When the tailor casts off on the next tack, the jib sheet will flow smoothly through the blocks and around the mast.

Of course, when the cockpit is completely awash in high seas, flaking the jib sheet is impossible. In those trying times I always glanced down at my feet to make sure the line was not wrapped around one of my ankles. I suppose if that had occurred my foot would have been severed before I knew what was happening.

Back on the handles and ready for the next maneuver. The rhythm continues.

14
Shapes

The glorious, feline curve of the jib was the most dominant shape of our 12-meter while under sail. We often talked about sail shapes, that is to say, how to adjust the shape of the sail through various on-board means so that our craft will realize the most speed. I was constantly amazed at how the minutest adjustment could produce a noticeable change in speed. Russell, more than anyone, had a precise eye for creating the proper sail shape. He was always fiddling with the jib leads, adjusting the outhaul tension, easing or tightening the jib sheet.

Sustained focus. Attention to detail. That's how champions win races. Any sport. Any era. Sustained focus. Attention to detail. Russell had it.

We went sailing today with only one minor problem: very little wind. It was cold and raining too.

"Maybe there's some wind out in the ocean," Cayard said.

Blackaller was off raising money, which suited everyone fine.

We left the Golden Gate Bridge behind at a surprisingly quick pace and sailed toward the buoy at Bonita Point. When we tacked around the buoy, we discovered there had been ten knots of current pushing us out to sea. At that rate we would have made Japan in about a week. We hooked up with the tender for the long drag back to the harbor.

We sailed around the bay for a few hours in a half-hearted way, talking about general sailor things: wind and tide, hull shapes and sail shapes, breast shapes, the usual.

A big part of this game was being patient, waiting for the wind, waiting for some part to be fixed so we could go sailing, waiting for the woman who delivered the lunches. Too little of my total time was spent engaged in some great, exciting sailing experience, but when those wild times occurred, I would ride that passion for a week.

Finally we returned to the club and washed the boat. Then we sat around and talked about sailor things again.

15
Day Off

My teammate and friend, Russ Silvestri, walked into the Bay Club a few minutes after I arrived and asked if I would help him move his gear from his old apartment in San Bruno to the team's new condominiums in Point Richmond.

Ouch.

A day off down the drain. I had planned to the minute how to pluck this rarest of syndicate birds: one of only a handful of authentic days off since I had arrived in San Francisco. But after a few moments I agreed to help Russ.

We had become a good port trimmer/port grinder team within our squad. In the thirteen weeks that we had been teamed together I had learned to anticipate his orders, and our on-board language had evolved into crisp, succinct tones. We worked well together. I was always amazed at the brutal honesty with which Russ approached life, work, sailing, women, pretty much everything. For instance, if he made a bad castoff with the jib sheet and as a result I was slapped on my forearm, he was the first to acknowledge his error. He didn't waste time apologizing. That wasn't necessary. He would say, "My fault. You okay?" And then would go on with his business before I could answer.

Russell was a good guy, and I hoped to maintain a friendship with him after the Cup. He reminded me of myself when I was his age, twenty-three years old. Russ did not suffer fools at all, and he wielded phrases like, "Why don't you get a clue?" at anyone who fell below his rarefied level of expectation. He could also be counted on to try his absolute hardest in every battle. That made him special. Russ was smart and determined, and he put some real soul searching into his sailing, exactly as I did when I rowed. His success came through pure hard work and nothing else.

He once told me a fantastic story about the time he had jumped off the Golden Gate Bridge. Around midnight, at the tail end of a drunken debauch, he climbed over the railing of the Golden Gate Bridge where some restoration work was under way. Then he pulled himself, hand over hand, through a maze of girders until he was directly beneath the actual roadway. Then he closed his eyes and jumped, right into the safety net that had been installed for the restoration work.

It's just like jumping off the bridge" he said, "except you only go twenty feet instead of two hundred."

Russ had been dealt a bad hand during the 1984 summer Olympics. He had won the Olympic Finn trials, officially fair and square won the trials, until the next best Finn sailor in the country (actually the third best Finn sailor), John Bertrand, filed a protest. In a last-ditch effort to gain a berth on the Olympic team, John Bertrand accused Russ of unsportsmanlike conduct in the final race. Russ had intentionally crossed the starting line early in order to prevent Bertrand from placing high enough in the race to dislodge Russ from first place overall. This is a common strategy in yacht racing, and is not considered unsportsmanlike. Weeks of desperate legal combat followed the protest, during which Russell was issued credentials and outfitted like an Olympian.

Only days before the opening ceremony, Bertrand won his case and Russell was fired from the Olympic team. The results from the Finn trials were reshuffled so that Bertrand leapfrogged over the second-place finisher and onto the US Olympic team. A long and complicated book could be written about what I just summarized in a few lines. The end result was simple: Russell was out and Bertrand was in.

A dark cloud hung over Russ for months after the Olympics. This 12-meter adventure marked a new beginning for Russ, and after the Cup he planned to launch a 1988 Olympic Finn campaign. I wished him luck.

A special bonus waited for Russ in Fremantle: John Bertrand joined the America II syndicate after the 1984 Games, and now Russell couldn't wait to pummel his enemy. In anticipation of that day Russell frequently directed a few well-chosen words at Bertrand's Olympic silver medal, which rested in the St. Francis Yacht Club trophy case.

Among other talents, Russell was the undisputed master of the sailor's hand jive. Left hand was one boat, right hand the other boat, and each hand moved independently— tacking and jibing, collisions and sinkings—like a funky puppet dance. Russ acted out the whole race in quick practiced movements along with a running commentary: "He tacked, I tacked and faced him, he tried the ol' slammerouni, and it didn't stick, I hit the left corner and tacked on the lay line and that was it, adiosi, seeyouinthebar." The race might have taken an hour or two. The story needed only fifteen seconds if it was close.

On the way to San Bruno to get his stuff, Russ told me an interesting story about the time he had two girlfriends, a French girl who lived in San Francisco and a USC girl who kept him company in Los Angeles. The two girls had never met, which was exactly how Russ liked it. Everything was fine until the French girl visited Russ at a regatta in Long Beach and his USC girl decided to surprise him at the same regatta. The two girls came head to head, face to face, claw to claw, immediately after the last race.

"Picture this," Russ said. "I was standing between the two girls, trying to take my boat apart so it could be shipped to Florida for a big regatta. I had to hurry because the trailer was leaving in an hour, and the two girls kept asking me to make some kind of loyalty statement.

"'Tell her, Russ,' they each kept saying, 'I'm the one you love.'"

And to confuse things further, Craig Healy (a fellow Finn sailor and now our navigator) needed a ride to the airport right away.

"I couldn't take another minute of the pressure," Russ told me. "I finally said I had to get some tools from my car, and instead I got in and left. I completely bailed out on the situation."

Russ finally settled down and called Craig Healy back at the yacht club to see how things were going.

"The two girls are comparing notes on you at this very minute," Craig said.

Finally Russ returned and finished with his boat. Craig and the French girl jumped into Russ's car, and the three of them headed for the airport, leaving the USC girl crying in the parking lot. Russ promised her he would come back in a few hours.

Russ drove to LAX and bid Craig good-bye. Then the French girl immediately went crazy and said she wasn't leaving. To make her point, she tore up her return plane ticket and threw it out the window. Russ became extremely weary of her about then, and he told her to get out of the car, right now. She wouldn't budge, so Russ went inside, bought her another plane ticket for San Francisco, and jammed it into her purse. Then he put her purse and suitcase on the sidewalk, hopped into the car, and pulled forward about fifty yards.

"Better get your stuff, or someone will steal it," he said.

The second she was clear of the car, he stomped on the gas and jetted away.

During the whole scene she kept complaining of chest pains: "'I have zee bad heart, Russ, so be gentle with me.'"

Apparently she was telling the truth. On the flight back to San Francisco she went into a mini-seizure, and when the plane landed a team of paramedics were waiting for her with a stretcher. When the French girl finally called Russ from the hospital to say she was dying, he said, "Have a nice trip."

That story needed most of the drive to San Bruno. When we arrived at his old apartment, we walked in on his ex-roommate, who was eating Raisin Bran and reading the San Jose Mercury News. The ex-roommate looked bad, sitting in a soiled bathrobe and wearing deck shoes with the heel part crushed down as though they were bedroom slippers. I avoided shaking hands with him.

I started carrying Russ's possessions out to the car, including the table on which his roommate was eating. Soon after we removed the table his old roommate got dressed and went off to work in a nice business suit and driving an orange BMW.

"He sells stock at Dean Witter," Russ told me.

It seemed to me he was getting a late start for a stockbroker.

Russ had exactly one vanload of belongings, which included a stuffed toy unicorn named Houdini that he had won for the USC girl at the L.A. County Fair some years back. He owned a hundred ties, several $500 business suits, a marble table and base that must have weighed two-hundred pounds each, a mattress and box springs of which we took only the mattress, two smelly bathroom rugs that we left behind, two peach-colored lamps with ugly round bases and fluted shades, a big heavy dresser, mustard-yellow and full of clothes that hadn't been worn in years. Everything looked tired and sad and boring, except a classy award he had received for winning the 1985 Finn North American Championships. I would have dumped everything in front of the Goodwill store and taken a tax write-off, except the award and the suits. Those I would have kept.

On the drive back to San Francisco I looked through a bag of pictures that Russ had accumulated over the years. I saw the USC girl and the French girl and a dozen other girls. The French girl looked much older than I had imagined. "Yeah, she's over thirty," Russ said when I mentioned this to him. I saw a picture of Russ dressed in a tuxedo for his high school prom and a similar picture of him in a tuxedo for his USC fraternity formal. His bow tie was much thinner in college.

It was a good day off.

16
Heads Up

Hurting. Let me say that again just to emphasize the point. Hurting.

We were racing the Heart of America and having a tough time of it. Yelling and strong wind added to the madness, and I did my best to keep my head down. The call was made to tack, and we had the handles going pretty good. This particular tack was different because we were switching jibs, and since Bruce and Scott Inveen were busy with that operation, Scott Easom and I were alone on the handles.

Everything was going well until I felt a mean slap on my forearm and then another on my chin and then a third, much harder shot to the back of my head. I was literally knocked down. Down and out. I must have lost consciousness for an instant because I don't remember going from upright to prone. I stayed down for a few seconds, assessing the damage, looking for the inevitable puddle of blood, trying to sense if my head was clear. No blood puddle formed. No protruding bones. Finally I decided that I was not badly hurt, although my jaw screamed like a fire engine.

The handles had stopped spinning—the tack completed—and I climbed to my feet. Russ asked if I was okay, and I nodded yes. He took the credit for having caused the accident by releasing his jib wire too soon, and I paid the price. This kind of injury is common in 12-meter sailing, and I was told I should not be surprised if it happened again.

I wish I had been the only casualty of the day's outing, but unfortunately Scott Easom, who was grinding on the starboard side, was also injured. Scott was our backup jib trimmer, who had been called into action when Oddjob and Jeff had business elsewhere and could not sail. Fifteen minutes after my flogging, we were about to round the windward mark and set the spinnaker when Easom was struck by the jib wire in a way that was similar to my experience—except Scott didn't get up. His eyes were closed, and he looked quite dead. After a minute he opened his eyes and said a few words, but still he didn't move. No one in the afterguard noticed our fallen comrade, and not until we rounded the windward mark did the news filter to the stern that we had a problem. After a few jibes and some discussion about Easom's condition, we dropped out of the race and turned for home. I'm amazed how blind Cayard and Blackaller were at times.

On the way in, Scott said a few words as the waves of discomfort flashed across his face. When we suggested an ambulance to take him to the hospital, he managed to say, "No fucking way." He changed his mind a few seconds later when he tried to sit up. Scott couldn't move at all.

About twenty minutes after the accident, we arrived back at the dock and then commenced another twenty minute wait for our team doctor, Dr. Enos Trant Andrews. We covered Scott with a towel and waited the long wait. Those few minutes were the most awkward I can remember: no one talked except in whispers, and I kept looking at the road, hoping to see the ambulance or Trant's Maserati. What was keeping them? I was glad to finally see the doctor walking down the gangplank.

After Scott left for the hospital I went to the dentist and had my jaw x-rayed. The dentist said my jaw wasn't broken and the sharp edge of the tooth I could feel with my tongue was not significant. He told me to have a beer and a few aspirin and that I'd be fine in the morning.

Dinner was a solemn affair that night. Toward the end we called the hospital to check on Scott, and the news was good. He wouldn't be sailing with us for a few weeks, but he would be back.

17
R-1, the New Boat

On Tuesday, June 3, the long awaited word raced through our morning workout: the new boat, Revolutionary One, forevermore known as R-1, had arrived. Time was now our most critical commodity: R-1 had to be on a freighter for Australia in seven weeks. In the meantime we needed three non-stop weeks of work to make R-1 ready to race. Then we would test her against E-1 for two weeks. Finally R-1 would return to the shed for fairing and packaging before the long freighter ride to Fremantle.

We ate a quick breakfast and then drove as a group to Anderson's Boat Yard.

Turning down Gate 5 Road toward Anderson's, the usually deserted parking lot looked like a small-scale swap meet. The Golden Gate Challenge directors stood next to their Mercedes while a KRON television crew and three or four still photographers directed their lenses on the huge white hull sitting on the truck bed. Even Ron Anderson rose to the occasion by not enforcing his parking regulations.

This was a good moment for the syndicate: the means for satisfying our dream had arrived.

Kenny was already hard at work as we piled out of the van. From this day until we loaded R-1 onto the freighter for Australia, Kenny was always *already there*. I've never seen anyone work harder on a project, and his ability to survive physically without suffering a heart attack or some equally deadly fate was testimony to his phenomenal inner strength.

Ron Anderson drove his Travelift at an exceptionally tame pace and deposited R-1 into our huge shed. We braced her carefully, and then Ron backed out and away. A half-dozen of us shouldered the sliding door and slammed it shut. Our clubhouse had assumed a whole new exclusivity, and I felt good being on the inside as a charter member.

I ascended the ladder, the first of countless times, and inspected our new boat along with every other crewman. A class of preschoolers climbing over a bright red fire engine could not have been more curious. We explored every inch, above and below decks.

I fondly remember Bruce Epke's curses echoing through the shed: "This is bullshit. This is pure bullshit."

The toe rails had been set six inches from the gunnel instead of one inch as he had requested, and he made sure we knew about it. I'd been around him enough to know that although he was justifiably angry, mainly he was exercising his cursing ability—something he practiced pretty much every day.

The secret to R-1, to our winning the America's Cup, to our getting our pictures on the cover of Time magazine, was contained in the very front part of the boat: a cavity for attaching a front rudder, known in the sailing and aviation business as a *canard*. No other boat in the history of the America's Cup had ever tried a canard. Wow! Score one! When combined with our missile-shaped keel, (soon to be the only 12-meter in Australia without a winged keel), we would have the most radical, high-tech, untested 12-meter ever constructed.

We all agreed, even those of us who knew nothing about yacht design, that R-1 would either be dog slow or blazing fast.

Scrunched into the darkened sewer around the canard-hole, we speculated on how this front rudder was going to be controlled from the stern. The canard-hole had been plugged like a wine bottle and painted like the rest of the boat so that looking from the outside the hole could not be detected. This was meant to confuse our opponents as to the true nature of our revolutionary beast. These tricks never worked.

I wish I'd positioned a camera on the ceiling and taken a picture every day until the boat was finished. The changes came fast and furious: winches added, steering wheels added, blocks bolted. Bruce ran a network of hydraulic lines underneath the deck to move the mast fore and aft and to perform a dozen other tasks. All the heavy work on a 12-meter is controlled with hydraulics.

We worked all day, well into the night, and three weeks later, on June 24, 1986, the R-1 was christened at the St. Francis Yacht Club.

The day after the christening marked the low point in my Golden Gate Challenge career. We had been told to report for duty at 6:00 the next morning, and at 6:13 a.m. Kenny Keefe saw me walking toward the dock at a snail's pace with my hands in my pockets. He pulled up short and berated me for five blistering minutes. He used every possible insult and obscenity, saying that my heart was not in the project, that I should quit, that he hated my attitude. He just plain hated me. I stood there and took it, half of me wanting to cry and the other half gauging the distance from my left fist to his sputtering mouth.

Every crewman eventually found himself on the receiving end of a Kenny tirade, and some felt his verbal whip on a regular basis. I had seen it happen to others, and it had even happened to me once before, yet nothing could prepare me for this onslaught. My first taking down had been a month earlier when I had also been late to work, and as before I soon felt only one emotion: a desire to quit. He might have been correct in that I had arrived a little late or was moving too slow considering the importance of the day, but one or two words to 'look sharp' would have sufficed. If he had something to say on a broader scale, a private dialogue would have been in order. These castigating sessions, the crew decided, were simply Kenny's method of management. If Blackaller could be likened to the slave owner, then Kenny was the maniacal foreman on our little plantation.

Not even Blackaller escaped Kenny's wild tirades, nor did syndicate general manager Ron Young, or world-renowned photographer Rodger Ressmeyer (our syndicate photographer), or the woman who delivered our lunches, or even Kenny's best friend, Hank Stuart. Only Kenny's wife escaped. The worst example occurred when Kenny mercilessly berated one of the land crew in front of the whole team and then fired the worker right on the spot. The team had watched the attack in frozen horror, as though a woman was being assaulted, and we did nothing to intervene. I felt bad for the man and disappointed at my own inaction for weeks afterward. I still do.

After a few months Russell and I were able to predict Kenny's outbursts, somewhat like dogs predicting an earthquake. We kept a healthy distance from Kenny during earthquake season, and our favorite saying when steam began to spout was "Here comes Kenny, and he looks pissed."

When my particular volcano subsided, I walked around the club a few times, decided to quit, changed my mind, and went back to work.

For two straight weeks we practiced on the smooth bay waters off South San Francisco. Cayard skippered the old E-1 while Blackaller naturally assumed the helm of R-1. Everyone wanted to sail on the new boat, but likewise most of the crew preferred to sail with Cayard. What's a crewman to do? As directed, I sailed with Blackaller.

Johnno Woultee, in charge of building and maintaining the new boat, became our twelfth crewman during the early testing. His hollow, bored voice would sound from under the decks at the very bow, "Twelve degrees, twelve point five degrees," as he sang out the angle position of the front rudder. That job rivaled bilge cleaning for pure unpleasantness.

These were the good practice days. For once my shoulders became sore from the volume of grinding, and I welcomed the feeling. Now we would get in shape and be race ready, and not a day too soon.

We needed two full crews to properly test R-1 against E-1, and we often recruited from the maintenance team for a missing grinder. Chugging through a tacking drill with our chunky machinist, Chris Rand, I was never sure if he was helping or merely resting his considerable weight on the handles.

R-1 seemed to be a little faster than E-1 during straight-lined testing. Any kind of testing was difficult because the sails might not be equal or the trimmers might not be as talented. A hundred variables always seemed to alter the results. The tacking ability of R-1 was the main concern because she seemed to lose all momentum in the tacks and needed an extra minute to reach racing speed.

When R-1 raced E-1 in front of the yacht club's bay window, Cayard inevitably missed a few critical wind shifts if his E-1 looked to be ahead of R-1. Nothing discouraged a sponsoring yacht club faster than to see its dream boat losing to the old war-horse. By the end of the testing, the front rudder still baffled Blackaller, especially the optimum angle to sail when headed hard-on- the-wind. These questions would hopefully be answered with another month of practice once we reached Fremantle.

Before we could pack for Fremantle, we had a small project to complete: the fairing of R-1.

18
The Fairing Party

Fair means even, like Blackaller and Dennis Conner stripped naked and wrestling in a wading pool full of thick oily mud. If properly advertised, one could sell a few ringside tickets to that fair fight.

That interpretation of fair was lost during the days from July 21 to August 7, 1986. For those two-plus weeks, *fair* meant that the hull of our new R-1would lose its subtle ridges and emerge from the shed as smooth as a pocket mirror.

Only one method is ever used to make a boat *fair*: long boarding. For centuries, boat workers have cursed this last great bastion of hand work. No machine can replace the human hand-eye-hand combination.

Our syndicate's diminutive, frog-voiced painting-and-fairing expert, Mark *Coz* Cosby became the unlikely general to lead us into battle. That first evening he gave us a lesson, Fairing 101.

"This is a longboard," Coz said, holding aloft an eight-foot-long, eight-inch-wide strip of plywood with two pairs of handles attached to the back.

The surfers in the crowd made some reference to longboards as a medium of wave riding, and Coz said curtly, "That's right, get the longboarding jokes out of the way now. I don't want to hear them again."

A few of us exchanged quick glances. A new and cold-sobered Coz stood before us. I had never seen him remotely serious in the months we had lived and worked together (nor 100% sober). I welcomed the change.

Next Coz demonstrated proper glue application. He grasped a tube of faux Elmer's and drooled a generous white worm over the front of the whole longboard. Then he unfurled a roll of thirty-grit sandpaper, tore off an appropriate length, and fixed it to the waiting board. Coz lifted the sandpaper in quick motions seven or eight times until the glue formed a cobweb of adhesion.

"No matter how hard the board scrapes across the hull," he promised, "the sandpaper will never budge."

"Always vary your strokes," he continued. "Use diagonal strokes, left-to-right strokes. Don't sand in the same direction more than twenty times or you'll cut a groove in the hull. Those are hard to get out."

Coz and Johnno manned the now-loaded longboard and set to work on the hull. They stood side by side, their hands moving in forced synchronization like hyperactive puppets as they scratched the sandpaper against the hull. The longboard working against the hull made an unpleasant hissing noise.

Within a minute a cloud of fine powder enveloped Coz and Johnno. The particles danced in the late evening light and then settled toward the ground. I could already tell I was not going to like this.

"It's a good idea to wear a dust mask," Coz said, although he had neglected to wear one. "Johnno, why don't you run to 7-Eleven and get some chips and salsa and a case of beer."

Coz was trying to lure us into staying, but I wasn't interested. If fact no one was tempted, except Stevie Erickson.

Stevie climbed onto the scaffold, and now, his chubby legs dangling over the wooden planks, a dust mask perched on top of his head, wondered who would join him on the other end of his longboard.

"Come on, guys," he said. "Let's do an all-nighter."

He was one enthusiastic bastard that evening, but for once he couldn't infect the rest of us with his spunk. I knew what was ahead. Even my untrained eye could see the undulating waves of work running from bow to stern. I wanted to pace myself as I would in a marathon. Only Stevie stayed behind.

We arrived at 7:00 the next morning. By 9:15 I knew everything about fairing. Everything. Luckily I had a good partner in Craig Healy. We took a conservative approach to fairing, keeping a steady pace, while other teams used a jackrabbit approach. Basically, any approach didn't much matter. We all sanded. We all suffered. The powder lodged in the corners of our eyes like chips of mosaic. The dust sifted through our masks, clogging our noses and throats as though we were lifelong chain smokers.

We all wore white paper suits, white dust masks, and goggles if we could find them. A T-shirt wrapped bandanna-style over your head or a cotton dust hood completed the uniform for our ghostly team. Only our shoes remained unique, and slowly they turned powder white.

At first I jokingly said to Craig that I wanted to hire someone to take my place. But after one day, I didn't say that anymore. No replacement could ever be found for a job like this. We would fight the eighteen-day war, (although when it began we had no idea how long it would last), in that odd bubble of hell, our shed at Anderson's Boat Yard.

Make no mistake, sometimes we had fun. The whole crew, eight two-man teams, would stand on the same hunk of scaffold and sand in unison. Our longboards would overlap as we counted the strokes in muffled tones until the command was given to switch direction.

One morning as Cayard was wrapping a T-shirt around his head, he said philosophically, "You know, I was driving to work yesterday, and I saw Blackaller's car in front of Christine's apartment. When I drove home thirteen hours later I saw Blackaller's car still parked in front of her apartment. In the same exact place. So while we faired, he slept in her bed, ate a nice breakfast, jumped her bones. He probably watched some porn on her VCR. Granted yesterday was Sunday, so he couldn't be expected to do much fund raising. But still it seems somewhat unfair. I drove a different way to work this morning because I didn't want to know if he was still there."

I wondered if Cayard was more concerned because Christine was a former girlfriend.

Blacky was seriously in love with this beautiful woman, which everyone agreed had a calming effect on our squirrely skipper. A rumor of marriage was confirmed when a jeweler called the syndicate office to check the billing address for an engagement ring.

Rumors and gossip and lots of cheap beer kept us upright and working during this gruesome fairing marathon. We didn't have the amusing diversion of seeing visitors march through our clubhouse. During R-l's initial construction, we had endured a score of visitors: the design team, Blacky, sponsors, donors, a seemingly endless parade. But we must have sent out a strong, threatening signal to all those people during the fairing party, because no one interrupted our fun the whole time.

As the days progressed, our uniforms began to disintegrate in cadence to our sinking spirits. The paper suits lasted about a week. We had been too liberal with their replacement in the early going, and finally the box was empty. We wore the last suits to tatters.

We survived on the worst diet known to man. Donuts and coffee for breakfast, lunch truck for snack, Little Louis two-pound sandwiches for lunch. Dinner was pizza and beer. Late-night snack was chips and salsa and more beer.

This endless slave labor brought forth the strangeness in us. We openly stole each other's chocolate chip cookies out of the lunch box, we hid in the container and paged through the latest Playboy and glued our favorite pictures to the container wall. We listened to Frank Sinatra on the tape player. Whenever *My Way* came around, we stopped work and sang along with Frank. Mainly we sanded.

Ten days after we started, a third of the fairing crew, led by Cayard and Russ, left for Cannes, France, to compete in a regatta. A day later a few more teammates left to take care of unfinished business now that our departure for Australia was near. In true worker-ant style, I stayed. And faired. All day long.

PART II
FREO

19
38 Hours in Transit, SF to Perth

"Como esta," the passenger behind me said to the young man sitting next to him.

"Huh?" the young man said.

"Como esta?" the passenger repeated.

"Sorry," the young man said, "I don't speak Hawaiian."

When I approached the flight attendant hoping to improve my seating position, she wasted no time putting me in my place.

"Upgrade?" the attendant said in response to my query. By her tone I sensed she thought I had asked to pilot the plane.

"Yeah," I said. "My ticket says I'm supposed to be upgraded to business class if there's room."

"Upgrade?" she repeated. "There's no upgrades here! Take your seat."

As I entered the plane I noticed a few empty seats just to the left of the doorway, the coveted business class. These seats had beckoned me with promises of free champagne and little socks for my swollen feet. I instinctively drew toward these corpulent recliners until the flight attendant grabbed my collar and shoved me into coach class, snapping the curtain shut. No upgrade today.

Hot and humid in the plane. Spooky too. Plane rides are getting spooky. Too many strange-looking folk are flying these days. Where do they get the money?

Three of my fellow Golden Gate Challengers were hiding somewhere on this plane, in business class perhaps, I couldn't be sure. My visit to that great land had been too short for a proper census. If only I had been on time. Having been aware of the 8:50 p.m. departure time for two full weeks, I stepped across my plane's threshold at 8:59, with a dozen seconds to spare. I've never seen one leave early, I kept telling myself as I ran to the gate from the security checkpoint, unless I counted the time at the Orange County Airport when I missed the flight to San Jose because the plane backed out of the loading area five minutes before the appointed takeoff time. Sure enough, that plane actually departed, wheels kissing the Tarmac good-bye, at exactly the scheduled time of 9:05 a.m. That airline's punctuality cost me a job at Wells Fargo Real Estate Investment Group. Just as well. If I had been hired by Wells Fargo, I wouldn't have been here.

"Two thousand three hundred and ninety-eight travel bank miles will be awarded in this flight," my attendant friend said over the public address system.

"Flight time to Honolulu will be..." She recited this information with exquisite timing, saying the first part and then taking a little break, just long enough to yell to the navigator: "Hey Naviguesser, how long to Lulu?" Then she demurely finished her sentence, "four hours and thirty-four minutes."

"The oxygen mask doubles as a flotation device," she continued. "No, sorry, the seat cushion doubles as a flotation device."

After crash-landing in the middle of the Pacific Ocean, I imagined, either device would be equally effective. Disneyland might want to consider a new attraction: the Emergency Landing Ride, where patrons slide down the chute into the waiting mouth of Jaws the Shark.

I had celebrated my farewell from San Francisco with breakfast at Fred's Place Café in Sausalito. Fred's is like a dinner theater with only one show ever playing: the Dance of the Fry Cooks. My favorite artist commanded center stage this morning, a six-foot-tall woman, Mill Valley High class of '69. She spun around the grease-laden floor with her spatula in hand, flipping the pancakes, sprinkling cheese in the omelets, singing a few lines to Fred. The whole performance was perfectly choreographed and executed. When I happened to meet her a month ago in the nearby Big G Supermarket, she was wearing a leather motorcycle jacket and smelling like warm home fries. Magnificent actress.

Fred's was not self-serve, nor was it cheap. Seven dollars for one person was the average cost, but the food and entertainment easily outweighed the expense. The owner Fred cut a dashing figure with his heavy Austrian (not Australian) accent, a fantastic wide grey mustache, and a USA America's Cup syndicate T-shirt that he wore whenever cooking. I liked Fred. He was a cool cat. He was also one of our biggest fans. He came to the freighter the day we loaded the boat. He stood off to the side by himself, just watching. As I left today he said, "Beat da pants off 'em."

After breakfast I called my best friend, Scott Roop, and said good-bye.

"I'll see you in March or April of 19-something. Not for a long time."

Then I drove to the Golden Gate Challenge office at 3737 Buchannan Street.

Oh, such a bummer entering that bastion of bad vibes. Cayard won his race in Cannes. That was good news. Everything else annoyed me. I was told to *pull my weight*, but not by Kenny or Blackaller. I was told by Blackaller's twenty-year old daughter Lisa Blackaller.

I survived thirteen years of elite rowing, made two Olympic teams, won an Olympic gold medal. Most lately I had endured six months of non-stop slave labor. And now this little shrew was telling me to *pull my weight*.

The problem started when Lisa, a junior secretary at the syndicate, had to drive "all the way over" to Brickyard Landing, (as though we hadn't driven twice a day for months), to make sure we had properly cleaned out our condominiums. Then she confronted the ultimate horror— a bottle of ketchup in the fridge and some cardboard boxes left in my apartment. She pointed her long witchlike finger at me and told me to pull my own weight. The image of slave-owner Colonel Blacky and the slave-owner's daughter Missy Lisa inspecting the slave's quarters slipped annoyingly through my consciousness all day.

I was in a far better mood once on the plane and drinking a beer. For the first time in my life I was flying from California in a westerly direction to Hawaii and beyond. Exciting stuff.

I do some of my best sleeping in airports. The three-hour delay in Honolulu was too much to take upright, so I stretched out on the floor and pulled a jacket over my head. For the next hour I slipped in and out of sleep as though on a teeter-totter with a playful sumo wrestler. Up and flying again. Lots of funny noises out on that wing, perhaps a few last-minute repairs as we taxied into position. Next stop Nandi, Fiji.

I ravaged the in-flight magazine rack after we left Honolulu, digging through every nook, but only Ms. magazine and Texas Business remained. Instead of reading, I listened to my new Book-on-Tape, Dr. Jekyll and Mr. Hyde—pleasant flying pastime. Fiji didn't look like much from the approach or sitting on the runway. No exiting was allowed. We sat and waited for thirty minutes until we finally departed for Sydney. I forgot to watch the water reverse direction in the sink when we flew across the equator. Next time.

Seven months into this adventure with five more to go—would the real, honest-to-God racing for the Cup make all the work seem worthwhile? Like almost everyone on the team, I had enjoyed a two-week break after the USA departed San Francisco on the freighter.

A few days of backpacking in the Sierra Nevada had worked wonders to improve my outlook on 12-meter life. The fairing party was already a semi-distant memory, certain to become one of those arduous battles that is spoken of with great affection as time passes. So far I considered myself ahead in the game: I now owned some of the finest yachting gear in the world, such as North Face jackets, Henri-Lloyd foul-weather gear, Golden Gate Challenge T-shirts by the handful, yachting shoes, deck shoes, dress clothes, a dozen hats, and even a piece of monogrammed soft luggage to carry it all. My 1984 Olympic outfitting was a Goodwill giveaway compared with the clothes we had received through the USA Challenge. The round-trip ticket to Perth with unlimited stops on the way home was a nice present that I planned to use to the fullest after the Cup was over.

Some of the more intangible things were still missing, such as that elusive team spirit that I was still counting on to make this America's Cup effort more than just a grueling year-long aquatic prison sentence. As soon as our team was complete and settled into that huge old house that awaited us in Fremantle, I was sure that we would finally start the team-building process.

Almost to Sydney and only 10:13 in the morning, but which morning? I needed a big, big map to sort things out.

For the first time in recent memory I suffered the embarrassment of fumigation. Moments after we arrived in Sydney two Australians armed with aerosol cans came aboard, and without warning they walked up and down the aisles spraying a thick glue into the air. Then they ran like rabbits off the plane. Some of my fellow patrons covered their snouts with hankies, while the rest of us just stared in disbelief. The bug hasn't been made that could survive that plane ride.

Into the final 250 meters, on approach to Perth, flying the inter-Australian airline, Ansett. A woman and her baby danced in the aisle, quick little moves— they'd been dancing since Adelaide. Every time she stopped moving the baby worked up a big breath and then uncorked a scream that would make Blackaller envious. Many stops since San Francisco: Honolulu, Nandi, Sydney, Melbourne, Adelaide, and now, thirty-eight hours later, we were on approach to Perth.

Touchdown.

20
New Home

I stood in the baggage claim area when a native guy noticed my brand new, ultra-cool, team issue, Golden Gate Challenge jacket.

"Oh, you're here for the Cup," he said. "We melted it down and made a plate out of it."

I was glad to learn these Australians had a sense of humor. Or maybe they did melt it down.

The first thing I noticed when I walked out of the Perth International Airport was Western Australia's version of

California's 1984 Olympic license plate. At the bottom of their license plate was the motto: *Home of the America's Cup.* Next to that a tiny outline of the Cup served as an exclamation point. The overall effect, bright yellow background with black lettering, long rectangular shape like the license plates in Europe, was very sexy. I was impressed. These West Australians were taking this little regatta seriously.

J.T. met us with a van and trailer, and we drove through the late spring evening to our new home. Unlike most international airports, none of the usual hotels, strip joints and cheap bars encircled the Perth International Airport. The surrounding countryside in an easterly direction was strictly barren outback and changed very little until you reached Sydney. Heading west along the main artery, Canning Highway, was a different story, with dusty suburbs, small factories, and used-car and motorcycle dealers crowding for space.

Finally we reached the biggest consumer of concrete and glass in the history of Western Australia: Alan Bond's looming casino/hotel complex, lifted straight from Miami Beach. Next to the casino was the Swan River, and a mile farther the city of Perth shone clean and new, with a handsome riverfront skyline like a scaled-down version of New York City. Canning Highway continued another five miles into Fremantle, but we turned off a mile early into East Fremantle—our new home.

Home at last. Our previous humble digs, the Brickyard Landing condo complex with a bubbling hot Jacuzzi and only one man to a room, could not have been more different from our new address, 6 Fraser Street, East Fremantle—a seventy-year-old, crumbling limestone house with walls sixteen inches thick and porous as a kitchen sponge. Our new home had been discarded by the America II and Australia IV syndicates when they grew too big or found superior lodgings. At first we had four or five men in each large room, although the attrition rate soon lowered the numbers. The married couples and female employees had a separate apartment house a block away. Our fearless leader Blackaller lived in some remote suburb whose location he refused to divulge, except to say he lived in a whole different postal code. And don't visit.

Our house had a fantastic corrugated metal roof, typical in Western Australia, that made a brief rainstorm sound like a preview of Armageddon. A portion of the surrounding yard became our volleyball court, and over the months we wore the green grass to brown threads with our evening jungle ball games. A myriad of bicycles, mopeds, and motorcycles found a home in the dirt parking area, along with a half-dozen Holden and Ford cars, the Sheik-van (shipped from San Francisco in a container), tender captain Mik Beatie's newly acquired Mini Moke, and, for a while anyway, two new Mazda vans. By the end of the Cup competition, we had collectively destroyed the motorcycle, several cars, the Sheik-van, and both Mazda vans.

My first chore was to find a bed. The early arrivals had claimed the best rooms, as was their right and privilege. Most of them had settled in the basement. We called those rooms the catacombs.

"It'll be nice and cool in summertime," Coz said, although right now the temperature outside never exceeded seventy degrees, and the catacombs usually stayed ten degrees cooler. Coz hesitated to offer me half his catacomb.

He had found a philosophical ally in our machinist, Chris Rand, and Coz had promised Chris half his underground nesting place.

I didn't want to room with Coz either.

I threw my bags on a bed in an empty room that had a nice big window and was close to the bathroom. A few days later I welcomed the addition of Russell, Craig Healy, and finally Scott Easom, my best friends on the team. But unfortunately the loud and constant television, located in the basement directly beneath my cot, made sleeping before 11:00 p.m. impossible.

After a quick tour of the house I settled down to watch the *Vice*.

Yes, it was Thursday, and that meant *Miami Vice* was beaming to every civilized country of the world. During the commercial breaks I heard the lowdown: no girls in Fremantle, but plenty in Perth, windy as hell every day, the work is hard with all day construction at the compound.

Stevie related this story that was presently racing through the Perth grapevine: a couple of guys on the Canadian team went sight-seeing in the nearby desert. Toward evening a kangaroo jumped in front of their car, and wham — one flattened 'roo. They stopped the car and took some pictures of the beast. Then one guy decided he'd take a picture of the 'roo wearing his syndicate jacket. He worked the little 'roo arms through the jacket sleeves, propped it upright, and took a snap. Next thing you know the 'roo came back to life. He'd only been unconscious, and now he was in no mood to sign autographs. The 'roo took off running for the hills, still wearing the Canadian's jacket.

The Canadian couldn't believe it, especially since his passport and wallet were in the jacket.

Score one for the kangaroo.

When I crawled into the rack, I could hear the ten o'clock news floating up through the floorboards. The weatherman was saying, "Tomorrow the weather will be fine." No elaboration or numbers, only "the weather will be fine." Everything was fine in Fremantletown.

21

Fremantle Reborn

My first morning in Fremantle I woke early and listened to the dawn, small sounds breaking the world of silence. This is my favorite time of day in any country. After a quick breakfast I borrowed a bike and rode toward the compound. I would rather have rested after my travel marathon, but it was better, I thought, to start off on a working foot.

Coasting down Preston Point Road to Riverside Drive, I pedaled on the bike path next to the Swan River. After a mile I came to an old brick building, the slaughterhouse. The door was open, and the workers sat on the ground outside, smoking cigarettes during their break. They wore white pointed hats and white smocks, or at least the color had once been white. Inside a man was pushing entrails into a dumpster with a snow shovel. Sea gulls perched on the roof and waited their turn.

Numerous graffiti slogans were painted on the wall next to the workers: Stop Live Export, Bury Hawke in Uranium, Save Freo—Give the Cup Back to the Yanks.

The last chunk of graffiti advice to *Save Freo* seemed the most interesting. It implied that something special was about to be lost. My cycling pace quickened—perhaps they were bulldozing the oldest aboriginal settlement in Western Australia to make room for a new Jack-in-the-Box.

I had seen this *Save the X* mentality before the 1984 Olympics, when people feared Los Angeles would capsize under the weight of the Olympics. It never happened. Games come. Games go. Life goes on.

The National Hotel and Bar stood two hundred yards past the slaughterhouse. Now I was in the heart of Freo. Those two words, *hotel* and *bar*, cannot be separated in the great country of Oz. Australian law requires a bar to be physically attached to a hotel, and there is no sense in owning a hotel if you don't have a bar to make it financially worthwhile.

Outside the National, a woman squatted in the gutter with her pants down around her knees. Her white bottom glistened in the morning sun. Small patches of cellulite looked as though they were stapled to her thighs. She was urinating.

A man stood a few yards away, his pants firmly strapped to his waist. He wore black boots, dark blue or black pants with a silver chain attached to a belt loop and connected to his wallet. His shirt had been black when new—now it was the color of thirty-weight motor oil after 211,000 miles. They made a nice couple.

The man was a Bog, the Aussie equivalent of Hell's Angels.

In the decades B.C. (Before Cup), Fremantle had been a tough little port town, with a bar on every corner, a few whorehouses in between, and overflowing with Bogs. These simple folk still frequented the National and the Federal Bar, two pubs whose patrons have never rubbed shoulders with the yachting set. Bogs have a boring fashion sense and untidy minds. They have seen our American biker movies, so they know how to dress and how to offer up the correct sneering facial expressions. But they don't have the right swagger. They lack the bulk to back up their drunken rages. Basically they're all actors.

Australia. I love Australia, especially the name. That name is cool incarnate, although I can't pronounce it like a native. They swallow most of the outer syllables, the end result sounding like ah-STROY-ya. The name can be shortened to describe the cool natives, as in Aussies. The true aficionado reduces the name even further, using only the first element: Oz.

Oz has borrowed a cultural odd lot from various countries. The roads were mostly finished when the first car rolled off an English freighter. That car happened to have right-hand drive, so for eternity the Aussies will drive on the wrong side of the road. The Italians have instilled a taste for gelato and a classical appreciation of la dolce vita. Only Italy has more public holidays than Australia.

I stopped at Gino's Trattoria for my first Aussie cafe au lait. The man who served me was a native Italian and an Australian citizen, and he accepted my money without a smile or a "thank you." Freo's strong Italian, Greek, and Bog communities were warming slowly to newcomers like me.

In the heart of town, the walking mall, old men sat on benches. A pudgy woman with three kids looked in the window of the Boans Department Store. A pair of red, white, and blue Docksides had caught her attention. These particular Docksides caught everyone's attention, and later I tried to buy a pair. They didn't stock size thirteen.

A young woman in the Benetton store turned over the *closed* sign. Now open for business.

A vintage bakery with giant Ho-ho rolls in the window called me inside. I bought one to complement my coffee and then looked for an empty bench.

Oh, yes, in the sitting position I could see what the graffitist had meant about saving Freo. Two main businesses were obviously thriving: the scaffold rental concern and the pastel paint concession. The train station was primed and ready for the final coat of soft pink. Six giant ceramic swans, three black and three white, lived in sculptured perfection on the roof of the train station. The swans had recently been painted, and now they shimmered in the morning dew. The post office was new and needed no improvements, except perhaps a few more clerks to handle the visitors.

Many of the old warehouses and offices had already succumbed to the painter's brush. The few remaining grey and brown buildings shocked the eye, like blemishes on Fremantle's nearly restored face. Not for long.

The Ho-ho roll was exquisite. I pedaled toward the USA compound with a hint of chocolate in my mustache and quite content at the changes taking place.

22
Compounding

Bare parking lot. Cavernous empty building. Long skinny dock. Taken together, this was our new compound.

We'd never had a proper compound in the Bay Area: the sail loft had been in Alameda, the boat yard in Sausalito, we sailed out of the St. Francis Yacht Club. Now we would consolidate everything into one simple compound.

I had no time to revel in my jet-lag stupor or even to enjoy the pleasant aftereffects of my giant Ho-ho roll. It was time to go to work. Our freighter would arrive in two weeks, and by then the empty building would be transformed into a professional sail loft and machine shop and offices for the syndicate staff. These prefabricated offices for Blackaller, our computer team, and the secretaries were already in place, elevated fifteen feet above the ground on steel posts. The offices had yet to be furnished, although that did nothing to prevent the constant use of telephone for calling family and well-wishers back home.

The bare parking lot would be fenced, painted. The choice of coloring was a pale off-green that Kenny Keefe chose to match the deck color of Courageous, a three-time

America's Cup champion. The color would serve as a little bit of inspiration, and I thought it was a good touch. I inevitably splattered my shirt while painting the parking lot, and although I cursed it at the time, that shirt with its strange green tint became my favorite.

The biggest compound-building chore had not started, although the heavy puzzle pieces had been acquired and showed a fine layer of rust as they waited next to the dock for installation. The air tanks and wet suits had been rented along with pneumatic tools. Now that the worker-ants had arrived, construction could immediately begin on an all-weather, x- ray-proof, ultra-secure home for our 12-meter — the safety pen.

Some good rumors were floating around Fremantle, such as the New Zealand syndicate owned a small submarine that had gathered an underwater photo of each challenger's keel. The Kiwis actually did own a small helicopter and even listed the pilot on their crew roster. With the translucent waters off Fremantle, a good view from the air was as valuable as an underwater photo. I never heard of any outright spying, such as in 1983 when a Canadian spy was caught inside Australia II's compound, perhaps because the current syndicates had too much invested to risk such bad publicity.

We had our own method for handling the spying-eyes problem: play pen, holding pen, pig pen—our safety pen gradually took shape and became all these things. The goal was to keep prying eyes from hassling our 12-meter beauty.

In this quest we were not in the least bit unique. But in the use of non-professional labor and every available moment, I believe we established a record among the other syndicates. Starting with only a skinny wooden dock and $22,000 worth of steel beams and corrugated siding, we created a long steel box anchored firmly in the mud.

I saw the plans, tallied the stock of steel siding (all of which would have to be attached underwater to the pylons), judged the total man-hours to be expended breathing bottled air, and then fell to my knees, thanking God that I had failed my beginning scuba diving class back at the Costa Mesa YMCA.

Stevie again championed the cause, and sometimes we worked together. I held a long steel pole, the bottom end stuck securely in the mud. Stevie, ten feet underwater, would position himself between the pole and steel siding. A huge stream of bubbles would break the surface as Stevie drilled into the siding while pushing against the pole for support. As soon as the bubbles stopped I would move the pole a foot farther along the wall. The safety pen took two full weeks to build, and at least four crewmen became ill from working underwater for so many days.

After we finished our first day's work, several of us pedaled along the docks to see what our opponents had devised. Every syndicate in Fremantle approached this prying-eyes problem with an individual flair. A quick look at a syndicate's compound and I instantly knew its money situation (or at least its ability to borrow), how long the group had been in Freo, and how many boats the syndicate counted in its 12-meter quiver.

On the low-budget, late-arrival side of town, (which included our syndicate), I saw the Eagle from Newport Beach. I noted longingly that they let it all hang out. No shroud or walls obstructed my view when they hoisted their boat out of the water. Only Eagle took this bare breasted approach, which I greatly admired for its simplicity, non-existent cost, and sensible attitude toward sailing. Eagle's small-dollar sponsors had been allowed to sign the keel with a felt-tipped waterproof pen. This was another good touch I admired. The super-chicken emblazoned on Eagle's flanks, however, eventually became its most dubious claim to fame. Eagle was soon nicknamed *Beagle*, and she was dog slow.

French Kiss, our continental neighbors only ten feet to the west of our compound, substituted a red canvas curtain where we used steel siding. Apparently they did not suffer for having invested so embarrassingly little time or money in their security system.

In the high-rent district, Stars and Stripes had adopted a US-embassy-under-siege-in-Iran motif. A former FBI agent had designed the security system, which included underwater motion detectors, a full-time security staff, video cameras, and even little plastic nametags for each crewman. We hired a security service the first month in Fremantle and had to wake the guard each morning to tell him to go home.

Alan Bond's Australia IV compound stood head and shoulders above the wealthy teams and ten miles above our humble place. Naturally they had the prime location, near McDonalds, the jetty entrance, and the Sail and Anchor Tavern. An insignia in the middle of their wrought-iron gate was stylishly shaped into the letters KA, followed by numeral 9.

Each 12-meter has a country code, KA for Australia, and a specific number. Alan Bond was betting a small portion of his wealth on KA9 and its ability to preserve his ownership of the America's Cup.

In theory, preventing someone from seeing our super-secret keel (code name *Geek*), and our ultra-super-secret front rudder (code name *canard*), would make them more difficult to copy. Of course both these things could be seen every time we went sailing. The front rudder rose into the air on any wave bigger than dolphin wake, and the translucent Indian Ocean permitted a crystalline view of the keel.

Suppose the enemy now possessed our secret information. Their design team must then discard their own now-worthless ideas in favor of the USA's appendages. This might prove difficult owing to the egotistical attitudes of all yacht designers. Getting two members of the same design team to agree on one original idea was exceptionally difficult. Convincing them to put aside their own ideas for another designer's creation was totally impossible.

When finished, we had a safety pen for baby—seventy feet long, fifteen feet wide, and completely enclosed from muddy bay bottom to twelve feet above the mean high tide line. At the far end was our drawbridge door, and in this style we differed from the other syndicates, whose doors swung open in barroom style.

No one illegally entered our pool, except a few nimble cormorants that slipped through a tiny hole near the back, and no litter ever escaped. Had we the money, I'm sure Kenny would have deposited a few hammerhead sharks into the pen each night.

For whatever reason, we never saw another front rudder in Fremantle, nor a keel even remotely similar to ours, the beloved Geek.

23
Alan Bond, in Search of...

Alan Bond was the whole reason we were in Fremantle and not in Newport, Rhode Island. I wanted to thank him in person.

After ten days of nonstop work building the compound, we were granted a day of rest.

While some of the crew went go-carting and others went to the beach, three of us went in search of Bond. Alan Bond.

Stevie, Jeff Littfin, and I climbed aboard our team-issue, white, one-speed Nishiki Landcruiser bicycles, and took off for Perth. We had the right day, clear and warm, as though the sky had been washed all night by an army of angels, so beautiful you wondered why there was a single problem in the world. It was a day for exploring and for loving life. Days like this help keep the ballast out of your soul.

Perth is a healthy bike ride from Fremantle, and we packed a lunch of three oranges, a can of Lemon Squash soda (*A Man's Drink* the label says), a Snickers bar, and a peanut butter sandwich just in case we became lost in the outback. We rolled out of the driveway, three ugly, mean, tough 12-meter sailors, yet looking suspiciously like thirteen-year-olds on their way to Mill Valley to have a chat with the Grateful Dead's Jerry Garcia.

Today we had Bond on the mind. His picture had been in every newspaper and sporting magazine after his beloved Australia II had won the Cup in 1983. He bore a striking resemblance to the English comedian Benny Hill, and he was also rich beyond belief. Finding a man like Bond should be easy for three sophisticated urbanites like us.

We rode along Canning Highway a few miles, more or less following the Swan River until it curved to the right. Riding over the Narrows Bridge, I saw the Fremantle Rowing Club tucked under the lee of the bridge. For once I wasn't tempted to go rowing. Sailing was too much fun. For a few minutes we stopped at a park and watched a couple dozen men playing the ideal Aussie game, rugby, aka football-without-helmets. Only Stevie was tempted to join the fray. Finally we came to Bond's Casino.

Bond, we figured, was most likely in his casino about this time of day, counting quarters and fitting them into little paper rolls. We parked our bikes in the underground parking lot and walked up to the escalator—perhaps the only escalator in Western Australia. We pressed our noses against the smoke-colored window and looked for Bond.

"That could be him behind the bar," Stevie said. "Let's go in."

We walked inside the sliding glass doors and made for the gaming room. Roughly a second later a security guard appeared in front of us. Oh good, I thought, a fan of the America's Cup. He must have recognized our T-shirts. Maybe we'll get some free chips.

"Sorry, you're not dressed properly for the casino," the guard said.

"Oh, some rule against T-shirts?"

"No."

"Is it the shorts?"

"It's the socks, actually."

"But I'm not wearing socks."

"Right. Socks are required if you're wearing shorts, and the socks must extend over your calves.

"Oh."

"He's all right," the guard said, pointing to Stevie, "but you two can't come in.

Stevie wore short pants, or poorly tailored trousers, depending on the viewing angle.

Stevie, I concluded upon our first meeting, was the most unlikely looking gold medalist in the history of the Olympics. He owed much of his gold medal to McDonalds. Before the 1984 Olympics he trained twice a day at that fast food dynasty and for one reason only: the more weight he carried, the better he could keep his Star sailboat on an even keel and the faster it would go.

Stevie was always smiling. I wish I'd known him before the Games, so I could tell if he was a changed man for having won his gold medal. I doubt it. He was always our happiest camper.

Stevie trimmed the mainsail in our boat—a job similar in importance to the throttle man on a steam locomotive since the mainsail was our primary source of power. The mainsail shape changed constantly with subtle wind shifts and little *flaws in the fabric of the wind*, as Blackaller liked to call them. For months Stevie sat on the aluminum crossbar in front of the powerful mainsheet winch, listening to Blackaller berating him, schooling him, chastising him, or scolding him. Stevie always came away smiling.

His proudest accomplishment since joining Camp 12-meter was having lost twenty-five pounds. He jumped on the scale every two or three days and inevitably screamed, "Hey-hey-hey," in a Fred Flintstone parody. "Damn, another two pounds." As he lost weight, he evolved into an exceptionally handsome man, and his charging-bull sprints to the foredeck to help get the jib down on mark roundings became an act of beauty. His only fear, now that he was losing weight, was of destroying his puppy-dog image that attracted the ladies.

Stevie had a somewhat limited musical vocabulary. He knew only one song, actually only one line from that song, but we could count on its recital at least once an hour: "Roxxxxxx-zzzzzzannnnn. You don't have to turn on your reeedddd light."

That drove me crazy.

The casino refused to admit the pride of San Francisco, so we remounted our bikes and headed for the Perth suburb of Claremont, where Alan Bond lived. After five miles, at the end of the bike path we had been following, we asked some folks where Bond lived. They said to keep on Galaxy Drive until it dead-ends, then stay right. Bond's house was about two miles away. A while later we asked a kid stuffing mailers into rich people's mailboxes the same question, and he told us it was only a mile farther. H even described the house—a green mansion at the end of the street. A young couple on bikes said it was only two blocks away. An old man dressed in white lawn bowling togs said, "Alan's home, I believe. Saw him drive up not too long ago." Everyone in Perth knew where Bond lived.

108

We found the vacant lot and then the street, Elwin Avenue, and coasted down the hill to the end. On the right was number 89, a big, green-roofed monster—ten thousand square-feet and completely encircled by a ten-foot wall. I looked for the doorbell, but before I pushed the button a security guard came over.

"Can I help you?"

"Yes, we're here to meet with Mr. Bond."

"Alan Bond?"

"Yes, Alan Bond."

"Is he expecting you?"

"No. Just tell him that Tom Blackaller, Dennis Conner and Rod Davis would like to pay their respects."

"I'm sorry, but Mr. Bond is having a nap."

"A nap?"

"Yes, a nap."

"What is your name?"

"Darrel."

"Darrel, did you say Alan Bond is taking a nap?"

"Yes. Perhaps I can tell him you stopped by."

"When he gets up from his nap?"

"Yes."

Bond, Alan Bond, the richest man in Western Australia, was taking a nap.

Nice neighborhood Alan calls home. It reminded me of the homes in Beverly Hills, only slightly thicker. They had a good river view, but their ocean view was nonexistent.

We said good-bye to Darrel and pedaled toward the beach. Nude sunbathing is a popular item around Perth, and we wanted to see for ourselves. In local terms we went for a *perve*. Wonderful word. Stevie saw seven breasts before I saw any.

24

First Hooting Day

Hooting means windy — very windy.

One sailor might ask another, "Was it windy today?" And if the wind had that special bite, whitecaps like popcorn scattered carelessly over the seascape, dry suit fully zipped up, one eye on the chase boat just in case he was to fall overboard or the 12-meter was to sink, then he would say, "Yeah, it was hooting."

On September 18, 1986, our third day of sailing in Fremantle, the wind was hooting.

The first day we had light winds, and practice was relatively easy. We had time to marvel at the crystal-clear water and enjoy our escape from the rigors of working. We were sailing and loving life. The second day the wind was about the same, maybe lighter. Today we had our first taste of the infamous summer wind known as the *Fremantle Doctor*.

When we left the harbor, the wind registered about twenty knots, the lowest reading we would see for the rest of the day. And the rain had not yet started. For three hours we tested different sails and tried a half-dozen straight-line upwind speed runs against Italia. During our final straight-line upwind test, the wind increased another notch. Toward the end a black squall marched over the horizon. In roughly ten minutes all hell was going to break loose.

We turned downwind, the direction of home, and hoisted our one-ounce billboard spinnaker. Before it reached the top mark the wind tore it to shreds. A few of us jumped forward and stuffed the remnants down the hatch like so much confetti. A moment before this $10,000 spinnaker had been exquisite to see, like a rare butterfly. Now it was rags. Our sailmakers waiting at the compound were not going to like this.

Blackaller called for a heavier spinnaker, and this one flew like an eagle. We stormed down the waves, drawing back the spinnaker pole near the crest and then sheeting in at the bottom to catch the wave's momentum. When timed just right, we would catch the wave and surf down the face, slowing at the bottom and then gaining speed as we topped the next.

Toward the bottom of one huge swell we heard a noise like cannon, and instantly our speed was cut in half. This heavier spinnaker had exploded, and now the pieces whipped madly through the air. The salvage drill was on once more as we gathered the pieces and dumped them into the sewer. The two shredded spinnakers frantically stuffed below, each big enough to cover a basketball court, made a shambles of the sewer. Sheik, as always, cleaned up the mess within a few minutes.

After this last explosion Blackaller called for the tender to tow us into the harbor. We dropped the mainsail, and for once we didn't fold it on the tow back home. The wind was blowing harder than ever, and if a yard of sail snuck into the water the rest would follow in a blink. The whole crew hung on to the mainsail, hung on to the boat, and watched the numbers increase on the knot meter. We were well into the thirty-knot range by this time, and the rain and whitecaps made for a complete, fantastic storm.

A hurried parade of 12s were simultaneously making for the harbor, and we slipped into position behind French Kiss. I counted six yachts in the parade, being led by their tenders like errant children caught playing in the rain.

"It won't be long," someone said above the noise, "until we're racing in wind like this."

I couldn't wait.

25
Beach Run

Russell and I woke early and ran from the crew house, across the railroad tracks, through the big oil refinery, to the beach. This stretch of hot sand was like none other in the world: fifteen hundred miles long, the whole length brushed clean each summer afternoon by the Doctor. The America's Cup had no effect on this part of Australia, except to force it to endure a few more footprints from visitors like myself.

The offshore wind blew warm, dry air across the beach from the outback direction. This offshore wind would ease at exactly 10:33 this morning, and for a millisecond the air would be still. Then it would come back on shore as though repaying a debt, heavy interest expected. This morning's offshore wind picked up the stench from the sheep ship Ala Farok being loaded in the harbor. The smell spread over the south end of the beach where we started our run. Fortunately, we soon left it behind.

I could see Rottnest Island, originally called Rat's Nest, sixteen miles out to sea. We had motored over a week ago and spent the day exploring, during which I almost stepped on a dugite snake, ten times deadlier than a rattlesnake. Weren't the rats supposed to eat those things?

As Russell and I continued our run, we saw the Dingo Flour factory with its five-story red dingo-dog painted on the side. This sign was a landmark for two reasons: it could be seen twenty miles out to sea, and more importantly, it was Alan Bond's first sign-painting job. The sign, like Bond, has endured. Now he owns half of Western Australia.

A mile into the run we passed the Fremantle Surf and Lifesaving Club. The garage door facing the ocean was open, and a surf dory waited for its crew to get ready. In front of the club fifteen kids surfed ankle-snapper waves. I'd been running here for a week and already recognized some faces. The older folk probably never missed a morning. If they could survive a few minutes in the cold ocean water, I imagined they could handle anything thrown in their direction the rest of the day.

Unmanned shark towers appeared like silent watchmen every mile. The sharks were no doubt just beyond the surf line, polishing their teeth in wistful anticipation of a careless surfer or long-distance swimmer. A few days ago a windsurfing speed regatta was held a few miles up the coast, and as one competitor was trying to water-start his skinny speed board a hammerhead shark surfaced about five feet away. Quite a stain left in the water as the windsurfer took off.

Russ and I turned around at the rock cliff and headed back. The beach was Australian magic. Six-thirty in the morning and already a hundred people were swimming, the parking lot almost half full. Morning was beach time. No flies yet. Good spirit. A halcyon day, magic from the first moment we stepped onto the beach. Yesterday's wind sculpted the sand into funny little ridges, and the tide and waves had distorted the shore into giant mole hills. We ran in the soft sand that Russell hates. For years I burned my leg muscles on soft sand, so I had a feel for moving easily over the ridges. Russell struggled—he cursed and sank lower into the little ridges.

The surfers had their waves. Women ran with their dogs. Old people bobbed in the water, taking the salt baths.

"Swim?" I asked Russell.

"Sure."

We swam naked like little kids for a few minutes. Naked swimming in the Indian Ocean on a perfect new day with the America's Cup starting the next day, October 4. I could not have felt better.

26
That Sailor Look

I'd been trying to get that classic sailor look, but I just couldn't seem to get it right. The look was all over Fremantle, so casual yet perfect in execution. The French crews seemed to have mastered the look along with the

Italians. The look has nothing to do with sailing ability—it stood on its own merits. I would need years, decades perhaps, to master that look, assuming I could get it at all.

Head: an earring is acceptable though rare. Only Scott Inveen opted for the earring look. Sailors of old wore a gold earring so they could have some ready cash on hand to pay for their own burial.

Haircut: flat top, ninety-degree angle, and no sideburns at all — if you are really hip, you notch your sideburns a half inch above the top of your ear. Long hair is so far out of style it might never have existed.

Face: red. The sailor's curse is to have fair skin. The sailor always has a tube of sunscreen, but usually leaves it back at the house. But skin cancer is no joke. Numerous wrinkles around the eyes and mouth are standard issue. Twenty-five-year-old kids look like they are going on fifty. But I've seen some guys who have sailed for decades who look like they just stepped out of the mold — must be in the genes.

Mustache is acceptable; beards are few. Completely in accordance with the sailor's hygiene code is to shave only once a week. At least that's how I interpret the code.

Facial expression: cool, looks as though he has seen it all. Probably has seen it all. Been around the world so many times, he's lost count. Tried a real job once, working for his uncle's construction company; after six days he received a phone call from a boat owner in Bermuda who said he needed him right away; told the boss he was going to 7-Eleven for a cup of coffee and never came back. Paycheck is still waiting on uncle's desk.

Education: *will finish someday.* High school, college, elementary school—take your pick.

Watch: Seiko Yacht timer; Rolex Submariner for a few. I really wanted a Rolex a few years ago, wanted one so bad I snipped a paper Rolex from a beautiful catalog and taped it to my wrist. Wore it all day to see how I liked the feel of it. That paper Rolex cured me of my desire. Magic

Shirt: tennis shirt for everything from chopping into the lead keel with a chain saw to dining at the Royal Perth Yacht Club; the shirt must be embroidered with the name of a sailboat on which you crewed; the names sound like Hemingway's favorite bars: Bondi Tram, Sidewinder, Windward Passage, Kialoa, and the greatest maxi-super-gold-plated-sailboat ever to ravage the seas, Boomerang. If you have a Boomerang shirt, you have something special. Bruce and pitman Jim Whitmore had a trunk full of Boomerang shirts, one for every day of the month.

Shoes: Docksides or imitation Docksides; veteran sailors have feet shaped like Docksides. You see some very tired Docksides plodding around Fremantle; sailors who have survived a million miles of deep water sailing with only their Docksides and themselves intact refuse to let them go.

Casual clothing: Canterbury—the sailing equivalent of Levis 501 jeans. Zippered down the lower leg, knee patches, gathered elastic waistband, extra-bright colors; the red version looks as though it could march into a blood bank and give a pint. I had never heard of Canterbury until I joined the team. What else am I missing?

Hands: always working, coiling a line, turning a winch, grasping a beer. Have yet to see a teetotaler sailor, about the same chance of finding one as of winning the Big Spin.

Formal wear: new pair of Canterbury pants.

Duffel bag: usually espousing your choice of sails, North, Hood, Sobstad. Inside the bag is a nice nylon jacket also embroidered with a yacht name, your wallet with about $15, and a couple of French francs.

Sunglasses: the most important item to many sailors (while some I've met don't even own a pair). Preferred brand is Bolle or Hobie, except Hobies are made of glass, which can be a real danger in 12-meter sailing, where heavy objects fly through the air with unpredictable frequency. One hit in the eye and you'd instantly wish you wore a pair of sunglasses with plastic lenses.

That sailor look cannot be bought, and likewise it cannot be changed with a trip to the barber. The sailors walking around Fremantle look as though they have neon lights strapped to their heads. They stand out in a big way. The sailor look comes from inside. Generally it is a good look, a good thing to be, a sailor, harmless at worst, exciting to the ends of the world at best. Someday perhaps I'll glance in the mirror and see that I've been blessed with the look.

PART III
RACING FOR THE AMERICA'S CUP

27
Round Robin I
Race 1
USA vs. White Crusader

Ladies and gentlemen. On the green course, starting from the port side, with an overall record dating from 1851 of countless losses and no wins—representing the pride of the Empire—Great Britain's White Crusader. Entering from the starboard side, direct from San Francisco, the untested, super-secret, super-fast, the name says it all, USA. Starting time 1:15 p.m. give or take a few minutes.

Race day had finally arrived, along with a nasty storm that was in the process of crashing our coming-out party like drunken fraternity boys, throwing their weight around and making whitecaps that stretched far into the horizon. I didn't envy the spectator boat customers who had paid $55 to escape from the relative comfort of the Sail and

Anchor Tavern, where the race was being shown live on television, to wallow at the mercy of the rolling waves.

On the Trojan Lady our syndicate women were taking turns sprinting from the cozy interior, out the sliding glass doors, to the transom where they assumed the classic position: legs spread, hands on the railing, head down, jerking in racked convulsions to mal de mer. The chumming tendency among the ladies was directly counter to the crewmen. Not a single member of our sailing team ever became seasick, either in San Francisco or in Fremantle. I felt queasy once when I had remained below decks on a riotous tow from the harbor to the race course during an extra rough day. Once I crawled on deck, the queasy feeling passed.

We had more important things to worry about than a little upset stomach. This first race had preoccupied our every waking moment for months, yet somehow we managed to arrive at the starting line fashionably late. Luckily it didn't matter. The race was postponed thirty minutes because no one could find his desk or the right classroom or even be sure he was at the right school.

To clarify: two regattas were being held at once: the Challenger regatta and the Defender regatta.

A total of thirteen challengers were begging, praying, and spending obscene amounts of money to get into the America's Cup Finals, where they would take on the Australian defender. On the other side of the equation, six Australian syndicates were also doing battle for the right to defend the America's Cup.

The Challenger regatta was organized by the Costa Smeralda Yacht Club. The world's richest man, Aga Khan, was a CSYC member-in-good-standing, and he provided, among other things, the legendary *Kalamoun*, the most luxurious committee boat in the history of yacht racing. (Louis Vuitton, the manufacturer of exclusive luggage and handbags, was the sponsor of the Challengers regatta. Thus every possible buoy, committee boat, and press release was engraved with the distinctive Louis Vuitton logo.)

Three series of races would decide the challenger.

Today marked the first race of the first series for Challengers, Round Robin I, where each victory was worth one meager point. In Round Robin II a win would be worth five points. In December, Round Robin III, a whopping twelve points would be claimed for each victory. The four challengers who owned the most points at the end of Round Robin III would enter the Challenger semi-final round. That was light years away.

With thirteen Challengers, the race committee needed two race courses, Yellow and Green, on which to run the races. On each course three races would be run simultaneously. One lucky boat was given a bye on each race day.

The best way to describe the dock-to-starting-line operation was arduous or, better yet, death-defying. This was the first time our whole fleet—USA, Trojan Lady, Sourdough, and the rubber chase boat, had operated together as the fully manned Golden Gate Challenge team.

Every syndicate owned a rubber boat for one specific reason: when transferring sails, the rubber boat's soft pontoons could ram into the 12-meter—as was inevitable in rough water—and not leave a gaping hole in the side. Our rubber boat, alternatively known as the Rubber Duck, Rubber Trojan and Rubber Lady, was captained by sixteen-year-old Hogan Beatie, the son of tender captain Mik Beatie. Hogan was the envy of his whole class back at Tamaulipas Valley High School. Hogan's competent grip on the steering wheel was testimony to his amazing degree of maturity. He drove the Rubber Duck better than I could have done with a year's practice.

Sourdough, our thirty-foot converted lobster boat, was unique to our team. The Trojan Lady was too small to carry the extra sails we might need on race day, so we brought the Sourdough to caddy the sails and to serve as a back-up tender. When Cayard called for new sails, the rubber boat would zoom over to Sourdough, the sails would be lofted into the rubber boat, and then Hogan would race back to the 12-meter. Sourdough duty could at times be great fun—a few beers, an extra lunch, power tanning. When the water was rough, it was a wet ride.

Our problem on this first day had nothing to do with the Rubber Duck or any specific part of the team. Overall we suffered from the same lack of cool I had witnessed my first day in San Francisco, only now we the problem was worsened by eleven other syndicates bringing their own special brand of inexperience. Taken together, the whole thing bordered on Indian Ocean gridlock.

Then the rain started.

As the starting time quickly approached, Cayard tried to pass the lunch cooler from the 12-meter to the Rubber Duck.

Cayard kept saying, "Closer Hogan, a little closer," until Hogan nudged his craft into the USA's transom, but with just a little too much momentum. The jarring effect knocked Cayard off the transom and into the water, still holding onto the lunch cooler. Hogan throttled back, and Cayard grabbed ahold of the pontoon lifeline—the cooler now abandoned for the Sourdough to retrieve. An instant later Cayard was returned to the 12-meter, soaking wet and madder than hell. This was more like it. Cayard was showing the spirit I'd been hoping to see all along. Sometimes a little calamity is needed to awaken the fight within a man.

Ten minutes before the start Blacky sensed a stronger wind was due, and he called for a mainsail change. Even in the best conditions a mainsail switch was the equivalent of changing all four tires on your pick-up truck while wearing your best suit of clothes when you're already late for the most important job interview of your life.

"Let's change to the #20 main," Blackaller said.

The whole crew looked up at the #10, all full and nice and generally doing an excellent job of scooting us along, and wondered: Are you really sure you want to change mainsails?

This time the change went smoothly, and when the cannon sounded for the ten-minute warning the whole USA contingent was ready. Both USA and White Crusader paraded from their respective ends of the starting line. We were cautious in our prestart maneuvers, this being the first day of school, but still the initial jousting went in favor of the USA. With a minute until the gun, Blacky luffed up nicely to the starting line with the Crusader on his leeward shoulder. With only thirty seconds to go both boats peeled off for the leeward end—Blacky had the favored position and forced White Crusader to sail lower than its skipper wanted. We tacked immediately before the start, crossed the line, and took off for the windward mark.

The shape of the America's Cup race courses is a common sight down here, having been printed on every cereal box, T-shirt, billboard and poster. Imagine an isosceles triangle, with the long base of the triangle pointing directly into the wind. The downwind angle serves as the starting line. The upwind angle serves as the windward mark. The boats sail from the starting line to the windward mark. Around the windward mark and then back to the leeward mark that is placed a short distance from the starting line. Once again the boats head upward to the windward mark. After rounding the windward mark we take a little sightseeing tour to the reaching mark off to the left side of the course.

That was fun. Now back to the leeward mark. Up to the windward mark, down to the leeward mark. Finally up to the windward mark, which has been magically transformed into the finish line. There are eight legs to a race. This can be an all-day affair if the wind is light, or home before *Wheel of Fortune* if the wind is hooting. The five-hour time limit ensures that sleeping accommodations won't be needed on board the 12s. In the whole regatta the time limit was never imposed.

The standard 24.5-mile, eight-leg America's Cup race course can be shortened, usually to three or six legs if there is too little or too much wind. If you have a good lead, then 24 miles seems much too far—why not 14 miles or 1.4 miles? If you're behind but catching up, the course seems unfairly foreshortened—at least 124 miles is necessary to sort out the differences between boats. The worst possible occurrence: to be way, way, way behind makes you curse the Everest-like proportions of the race course. In these instances the water turns to glue—nothing good can come of a long, losing effort. Invariably you hate sailing and wish something would break so you can go straight home.

As we feared, on the first upwind leg the White Crusader powered ahead of the USA and was cruising nicely until suddenly its mainsail dropped from the top of the mast. Bad luck. They sailed with only a jib for about five minutes, until their mainsail went back up the mast, where it stayed the rest of the afternoon. But while their mainsail was taking a breather the USA powered ahead of White Crusader, and around the first windward mark the two 12s were separated by only inches.

The battle stayed hot the whole afternoon; Crusader would pull ahead on the windward legs, but we would regain on the downward slides. The lead changed hands five times before the last leg. Going into the last two-mile stretch, Blacky tacked like a madman, looking for an opening, a mistake by Crusader, any possible way to get our bow in front before the finish line. But after twenty-four miles of racing we came up nine seconds short. Our first America's Cup race went to the pride of the Empire.

The mood at dinner that evening was spooky, mainly because no one seemed too concerned that we had lost. The real urgency centered around getting a jumbo plate of food and then retreating to the television room to watch *Cupdate*. This half-hour locally produced show was destined for greatness, at least among the crewmen. Tonight's *Cupdate* featured our race since it was close to the very end.

Blacky didn't attend dinner, at least not at 6 Fraser Street. Except for when we actually went sailing, he had been missing since the night Christine flew into Perth.

28
Round Robin I
Race 5
Battle of the Rivals

So far, not so good. In the second race we defeated Courageous, a yacht that should have been in a maritime museum rather than limping around the Gage Roads race course. Against New Zealand in the third race we accidentally stumbled over the starting line early, handing them a one-minute lead that we never came close to overcoming. Then we had floundered in the wake of America II, thus denying Russell his hotly desired revenge against John Bertrand. One win and three losses was not going to get us on the cover of *Sports Illustrated*.

In one short afternoon, however, we could wipe away that disappointing record with a victory over our great rival, Dennis Conner, and his slate blue Stars and Stripes.

Actually, Conner was Blacky's great rival.

Blacky, we all knew from a few thousand diatribes, hated Conner in a rare loathing that started dead-center in a man's soul and spread outward until every cell was infected. The passion Blacky expressed was final, complete, almost beautiful.

I knew the usefulness of a hate such as this from personal experience: during the 1984 Olympic year an invaluable enemy had spurred me through a whole season of the harshest training I could endure. In an overall view, I wanted to win an Olympic medal. But more immediately, I craved a victory over my enemy during our daily battles on Newport Harbor. '

Blackaller had it over Connor when it came to speaking the King's English. Dennis Connor had a high, whiny, unpleasant, downright off-putting voice. Tom Blackaller could speak with a hypnotic ease in front of the media, at fund-raisers, yacht club banquets. No crowd was too big or small for Blacky. Unfortunately Blacky's glibness didn't help when it mattered, on the race course.

Conner had won a 1976 Olympic bronze medal in the Tempest event. He was navigator and starting helmsman on the 1974 America's Cup champion. Best of all, Connor had skippered a successful America's Cup defense in 1980. Along the way Conner had also won all the prestigious big-boat regattas. Blacky's last major victory had been in 1981 at the prestigious Southern Ocean Racing Circuit.

Even that win was marred by the questionable rating of his yacht.

That was then, this was now. Our beloved USA had been measured and re-measured and passed the rules committee inspection. Now we could race. The huge door on our safety pen swung open, and we began inching the boat, hand over hand, toward the wide-open ocean. A sizeable crowd had gathered on the dock to cheer us on our way. A few feet beyond the safety pen a local television crew in a rubber dingy begged a few words from Blackaller regarding his prediction for today's race. Russell was extra-sharp today, and he beat Blacky to the verbal punch: "We'll nail his ass to the wall."

Once clear of the breakwater we angled toward the starting line, a mere speck on the horizon. Then we settled into our daily storytelling session. I took my place on the cockpit floor next to the grinding pedestal and leaned back, letting the words trickle over me like a soothing rain on a summer day. This morning Blacky told an excellent story about the 1969 Star World Championships: Blacky was leading the regatta with one race to go, but if his nearest competitor, Pelle Petterson (Cayard's father-in-law) finished right behind Blackaller, then Petterson would win. Toward the end of the race Blacky worked onto starboard—the tack with the right of way—and proceeded to drive over Petterson in steamroller fashion and get the victory.

Good story, Blacky, really inspiring. I was ready, all tuned up and set to grind, when suddenly the postponement flag was abruptly hoisted from the committee boat. The wind had not figured out its preferred direction. On Cayard's command we spent the next fifteen minutes shuffling sails between the Sourdough and USA just to make sure we had the right sail wardrobe for the changing conditions. The jib and spinnaker had about the same bulk and unwieldy quality of a twenty-five foot long basking whale. As the shuffling progressed we cursed having to drag them out of the sewer. We sail changers (pretty much the whole crew except Blackaller, Craig Healy, and Hank Stuart) always started the race with a good sweat warming the insides of our dry suits.

The postponement flag was finally doused, and we prepared to enter the ten-minute sequence that immediately precedes the start. With navigator Craig Healy counting down the last few seconds we swung into a hard reach to gain full speed. Both 12-meters had to stay outside and on opposite sides of the starting line until the ten-minute gun fired. After the ten-minute gun, we would be free to go anywhere on the whole Indian Ocean just so long as we were safely tucked behind the line before the starting gun.

We were on starboard tack when we crossed the line, and the whole crew predicted with lightning accuracy that our initial course would intersect Conner's midship. On that first pass we ranged close enough to read the compass on Stars and Stripes mast, and its whole crew turned and glowered in our direction. Naturally we glowered back, and I could feel the tension charge between the boats like two dogs preparing to lunge at each other.

The two boats immediately began the first of about twenty pre-start circles. We chased the stern of Stars and Stripes, looking for the elusive opening, trying to get its navigator so dizzy that he couldn't see the weather mark. For just a moment I looked to the opponent's boat to see if my friend Tom Darling was manning one of its grinding positions. Tom and I were teammates on the 1984 Olympic rowing team, and we both happened to discover this bizarre America's Cup sport at exactly the same time. I didn't see Tom, and I had a feeling that he was being saved for the heavy wind in December.

Both 12s finally ran out of circling steam, and we started a new tactic: luffing into the wind. This luffing technique is like sitting on top of a roller coaster, waiting for the inexorable fall. The sails snapped overhead like cannon fire, and only ten feet away another sixty-six-foot- long beast was making the same horrendous luffing noise.

At a minute to go we fell off to port with Stars and Stripes falling with us. We found a little surge of speed at exactly the right instant and nudged ahead. Then we tacked and went for the line, but not without Russell and Stevie offering up some heavy cursing on Conner and crew as we slipped away. The official Louis Vuitton record showed USA-winning the start by two seconds.

"Settle down" were the immediate watchwords from tactician Cayard.

Yes, good tactics, Paul. Brilliant. Settle down. We had become a little unhinged back at the start. A minute into the race Conner tacked right, and we tacked a moment later to provide the traditional *cover*. We didn't want Conner to fall into a better wind or some weird Madagascan current that would shuttle him into the lead.

For the next three hours we strained and worked and humped our beast over this Indian Ocean sweatbox, but as in the White Crusader race, Conner kept inching closer on the upwind legs while we pulled away on the long downwind slides. We could never distance ourselves to put them away for good despite trying every maneuver in the match-racing handbook. With barely eight knots of breeze to power the boats, conditions similar to those in Newport, Rhode Island, the skipper's strategy, rather than pure boat speed, played a huge role. Blacky and Conner schemed like demented chess masters, testing each other, looking for a crew weakness or a loss of afterguard concentration.

As we hurriedly prepared to round the second weather mark our usually sure-handed pit man, Jim Whitmore, accidentally let go of the halyard he was clearing. The look on his face that followed was pure disbelief as the halyard dangled off the port side of the boat, just out of reach. As bowman Scott Inveen retrieved the halyard using the bosun's chair, Whitmore muttered, "I've never dropped a halyard in my life." The tension was bearing down hard on everyone.

We kept our lead around the whole course, right to the last, tiny excruciating fifty yards. Then the wind shifted. It did not portend well. We tacked with forty yards to go, the finish line so close I could almost touch it. Now we were only twenty-five yards away.

The moment of truth had arrived. We were on starboard tack. Dennis Connor was on port. We had the right-of-way, and best of all we were on an intersecting courses. The obvious conclusion on either boat, to the helicopters buzzing overhead, to the press boats and chase boats and spectator boats hovering nearby, was that a big ugly collision was going to take place in exactly one second. The slate-blue hull of Stars and Stripes marched into my field of vision. I could see its crew hunkered down and bracing for the impact. Dennis Connor was at the helm, looking like a used-car salesman trying to unload a '67 Valiant. He looked sheepish and slightly unconcerned, comical with his zinc oxide smeared around his face like a lazy clown. Their mast cleared our bow, and now we shifted farther down the length of his boat. It appeared we would slam into his wheel.

Stevie suddenly jumped up and screamed, "Hit him, hit him!"

Their transom was now our last and only target. A good whack on their transom would take out their permanent backstay, and the Stars and Stripes' mast would come crashing to the deck like an erector set. Too bad, Dennis, you know the rules: starboard has right-of-way. This was the moment of truth we had all been waiting for. I gripped the grinder handle and waited for the explosion.

No explosion came.

Dennis Conner cleared our bow. Victory to the Stars and Stripes. Six seconds.

29
Round Robin I
The Last Race

For two weeks we had battled the world's best skippers, crews, 12-meters, and occasionally the Fremantle Doctor. We lost a few close races at first, but lately our win column had been filling up nicely with six wins in a row— every race since our loss to Stars and Stripes. If we could manage a victory over French Kiss, our place in the coveted top-four ranking would be secure. Overall, I thought our showing had been adequate considering we had a flaky skipper, a nervous crew, and a very radical boat.

Our humble compound shared a fence with the French Kiss compound, and only a drooping length of red canvas prevented our observing their every move. Over the last month I jealously concluded that the French Kiss crewmen were having a hell of a lot more fun that us, riding their high-powered motorcycles through downtown Freo while wearing full-length Driza-bone capes. They seemed too good-looking for real sailors, and whenever we weren't around they talked to our girlfriends. The French Kiss team had their own version of Kenny Keefe, who chased his slaves out of their sail loft and made them work when they preferred to pass the wine bottle. The French Kenny had long stylish hair and wore FILA warm-up pants, but underneath he was a mirror image of our own human volcano.

International relations between our two camps had been subdued except when we inexplicably tossed beer bottles into their compound or when one of their crewmen tried to sneak a peek at the Geek. But today we put aside our Politeness Man act and came out swinging. Our race promised to be a classic—the stylish, sophisticated French Kiss against the homegrown USA.

A few days earlier we had been scheduled to race the other French entry in the America's Cup, Challenge France. Unfortunately, one minor problem arose—they overslept and missed the start. Actually their halyard jammed as they tried to raise their mainsail on the way to the starting line.

As the rules dictate, we sailed the course by ourselves with only twenty-five knots of breeze to keep us awake.

French Kiss had nothing in common with Challenge France, except a similar language and that their respective skippers, Marc Pajot and Jean Pajot, were blood brothers although they supposedly hated each other. French Kiss had everything I would expect from a cosmopolitan challenger, including matching uniforms, worldly experience, and jet-set money. This same boat and crew finished an impressive sixth place in last year's World 12-meter Championships held here in Freo. The Kiss proved to be especially fast in heavy wind. The USA R-l was a mere gleam in our designer's eye while French Kiss was battling the Fremantle Doctor and winning.

Their major sponsor, Kiss Photo, a one-hour film developing company, received immeasurable publicity with the success of its namesake. The ancient Corinthian rule forbidding blatant advertising on racing yachts was severely tested at the start of this America's Cup by French Kiss and Great Britain's White Horse Scotch Crusader. Our former Pacific Telesis banner never found its way onto our new boat, thus we never had to deal with this problem. A little hassle might have been worth an extra million dollars for naming rights.

These restrictive rules were changed, effective after this edition of the Cup, to allow for unlimited advertising on 12-meters. A more natural billboard has never existed than the hulking 12-meter mainsail, or the graceful jib, or the bulbous spinnaker, or the boat itself. If Eagle had been sponsored by Purina Puppy Chow, it might have been able to afford a better design team. During the next America's

Cup the 12-meters will be so covered in sponsors decals as to make an Indy race car look like an anonymous taxi cab.

I was especially fond of one French Kiss peculiarity: neatly lettered on the hull, just below the big wheel on each side of the boat, was the skipper's name, M. Pajot. Not to be outdone, this morning Paul Cayard borrowed our welder's grease pencil and scrawled *T. Blackaller* in a similar spot on the USA. For a few moments the notion ran through our boat to write every crewman's name on the hull near his work station. Toward the bow we would have *S. Inveen—Bowman*. Our welder wanted his grease pencil back, so that plan was abandoned.

The die for the race was cast early with twelve knots of wind, light chop, clear skies, an altogether excellent summer day. When the ten-minute gun sounded, the USA strode through the line with all the confidence of a winning team on a hot streak. The pre-start maneuvering was timid except for a wicked luffing drill, a noisy test of nerves to see which skipper, M. Pajot or T. Blackaller, would veer off first. Blacky won that mini-game of chicken, but French Kiss won the start by seven seconds.

On the first upwind leg the USA marched underneath French Kiss, and we gradually pulled away to a sixty-second lead by the first windward mark. French Kiss was passionate about heavy wind, but this light breeze was intolerable to her delicate palate. For the rest of the race, seven more legs, the margin between the two beasts never changed by more than fifteen seconds.

Our crew work was excellent, no mistakes were made by the afterguard, the foredeck performed admirably, and the USA claimed the win. Welcome to Top Gun. We also beat French Kiss back to the dock, and we were minutes faster in getting our mast out of our boat. Basically, we had their number from morning croissant to late night cappuccino.

What did it all mean? With that victory the USA now sported a record of eight wins and four losses. Three teams had better records, New Zealand's Kiwi Magic, America II, and Stars and Stripes. Currently we were tied with the White Crusader for fourth place. Not bad.

Some of our opponents were obviously on their way home, or at least they should have been. I couldn't help feeling sorry for the crew of Courageous IV or Challenge France. Regardless of their expectations, losing is hell, and they had just spent two weeks shoveling coal in the darkest corner. In front of the Louis Vuitton race headquarters a huge billboard listed the results of each race: X marked a win, and O meant a loss. The O's ran long and wide in the Courageous column except for one beautiful X, where it had defeated its cellar mate, Challenge France.

I stayed late at the compound, washing sails and talking to my friend, sailmaker Jim *Chewy* Watters. Chewy and I shared a common love for backpacking in the Sierra Nevada, and we both knew that the closest we'd get to the Sierra this year was to reminisce over past adventures.

Long after dark I started my three-mile pedal home to 6 Fraser Street. The Fremantle Police had increased their rank by two or threefold in honor of the Cup, and when things got slow the cops would ticket unlighted night-bikers like myself. To give these sharp-eyed cops the slip I rode through the huge freighter shipping yard along the Swan River.

At the northern end of the shipping yard, farthest from the tourists, the 12-meters, and the fancy Esplanade Hotel, was the sheep ship Mawasi Tabuk. The Mawasi was all lit up, actually glowing with a cruel neon halo. She was six hundred feet long with an immense superstructure like a ten-story prison, the devil's version of Noah's Ark.

Fremantle is the western embarkation point for these huge ships—110,000 live sheep per ship, three days of nonstop loading to fill them up. As I stood along the railroad tracks watching the commotion, I concluded that there was nothing in the world, nothing in the whole universe, to compare with the smell of a sheep ship.

The sheep-hauling trucks were lined up in rows, with the drivers waiting silently to unload their cargo. When his turn came up, the driver backed his truck up to a ramp and lowered the tailgate. The sheep could barely walk after being cramped inside with 330 of their mates, and seeing them prodded up the long ramp to their new cells was bizarre fare for this midnight hour. The sheepdogs kept up a steady, high-pitched barking, three or four languages were being shouted at once, and above it all was the sound of a whip hurrying the dumb beasts along. Every living creature—the sheep, dogs, truck drivers, crewmen, stockmen, and I— knew that the sheep were on their way to die, and somehow that seemed to produce a biting, fetid smell that I had never experienced.

Live sheep export to Saudi Arabia is a big controversy in Australia. The Muslim religion requires meat to be freshly killed, thus the meat must be shipped live. Not surprisingly, animal rights protesters claim the long, two-week voyage to Saudi Arabia is cruel treatment for the sheep. A well-fed pack of sharks follows each ship like grim morticians, dining on the thousands of unfortunate passengers who die on the voyage and are tossed overboard.

Months later, after the Cup was over, I felt the urge to go aboard a sheep ship. I'm the first to admit that this was a strange urge, but I felt it too strongly to ignore. Our bowman, Dana Timmer, who somehow knew about these things, assured me I'd never get off the ship alive.

30
Little Creatures

Break time at last. We needed this time-out to return to our San Francisco roots: working on the boat. After two weeks of nonstop sailing we had almost forgotten our secret path to yachting enlightenment. Kenny the Tyrant soon insured that we remembered.

On the first break day Kenny posted a five-page, single-spaced list of projects with the initials of one or more crewmen carefully hand-lettered in the margin. The crewman who owned those initials would tackle that particular job. The mast repair team, led by Jim Whitmore, bent over the mast changing the halyards and replacing fittings, constant work under the hot sun. Under Jim Plagenhoef's direction each of the USA's dozen winches had to be removed, completely dissected, lubricated, inspected, and remounted—a full-time job for his three-man team. Russell and I were assigned to *sail patrol*, washing, mending, and folding the whole sail wardrobe.

From my first week down under I'd found a niche in the sail loft as an apprentice sailmaker. Chewy Watters and Olga Slawinski, our two professional sailmakers, taught me to operate the big sewing machines they had brought from San Francisco. Mainly I specialized in hand work, using the heavy needles and leather palm to attach various stainless-steel rings and lines to sails and sailbags. I loved working with Olga and Chewy in the loft. We became good friends, and now that I had a useful job, something I had been denied in San Francisco, the work days went much easier.

The fifteen-day break was like the recess between periods in an extended hockey game. Get out the Zamboni and smooth the course—heavy winds were on the way. The Fremantle Doctor was due back from vacation and he would be carrying ten billion whitecaps in his little black bag. Every 12-meter, ours included, would be tuned for heavier winds and rougher seas. Some boats, like America II, needed a little more work, but our beast was fundamentally okay, which was okay with me. I imagined most of the Challenge France crew was spending their break windsurfing or teaching the native women right from wrong the French way.

Around one o'clock on this fourth work day, Chewy, Olga, and I put down our tools, clicked off the sewing machines, and rode our bikes to the Fremantle Sailing Club for our regular luncheon appointment. We were temporary members of the FSC, along with the crews of Eagle, French

Kiss, and White Crusader, since all our compounds were located on sailing club property. The club was a welcome diversion from the daily work grind and a lively place to sample authentic Aussie life.

My first day in the Fremantle Sailing Club I stood in the bar, drinking a beer and talking to a fellow crewman, when a local sailor-drinker approached us and asked, "Would you mind telling your mate not to wear his hat in the bar?" I was wearing the hat, yet the man, standing only fifteen inches away, did not direct his query to me. Thus, before I had consumed two ounces of my ten-ounce beer (known as a midi—midway between a kid's beer and a man's beer), one of the great Australian drinking traditions had been brought to my attention: a hat is never worn in an Aussie bar. If someone should ring the bell positioned next to the cash register while I wore my hat, I would be obligated to buy a round of drinks.

This afternoon the hatless Chewy ordered a pitcher of beer and three glasses. We drank our beer and ate our personal favorites from the lunch line. I ate a huge plate of vegetables, rice, and French fries (called chips).

During my first month in Oz I helped start a new tradition in the FSC dining room. With the approval of the cheerful ladies behind the counter, I tossed a handful of Snickers bars into the ice cream freezer. Within minutes my duty to the culinary advancement of Australia was fulfilled: the first frozen Snickers bar ever seen below the equator.

A few minutes after we arrived, Kenny and Hank sat at a table and began eating. We were soon joined by Russell and Bruce. Then Mik and Hogan walked in and ordered another round of beer. Within twenty minutes every member of the crew—sailors, designers, on-shore workers, painters, welders—everyone except Blacky—sat down together, drank beer, ate their lunch, and talked.

A few hundred yards away, our beloved USA rested in the noon sun while we embarked on a fantastic afternoon. For two hours we talked about every problem in the syndicate. We talked as friends and respected teammates. We drank beer and ate chips with vinegar and hot mustard.

In this one afternoon we came closer to being a team, rather than a loosely associated group of individuals, than in the whole time we'd been together.

Work was officially abandoned for the day, and we all piled into the vans and drove south out of town to the largest go-cart track in the southern hemisphere. I drove with Sheik, and when we accidentally passed the go-cart track entrance Sheik threw over the wheel in a wild U-turn. Jeff Littfin, sitting in the passenger seat, suddenly fell backward with a loud crash and scream. His seat was completely upturned, and he remained frozen, eyes fixed on the roof, due to his tight seat belt. Somehow he survived.

By this time our syndicate had a ten-man support crew, whom I dubbed the *Little Creatures*. Mainly they were of a smallish stature, except Chris Rand. During the break our Little Creatures proved to be the heart of the whole program. They worked all day and all night for days on end. I honestly do not know how they survived. I don't want to know. But they seemed to work all the time. Johnno Woultee was the king of the Little Creatures. He was the smoothest, most controlled individual I have ever seen, working like a blue-jeaned ballet dancer, never hurrying or wasting motions. His work was meticulous, fine, and surprisingly fast. Chris Rand, the machinist, was Johnno's right-hand man. Professor Phil Kieko served as liaison between the designer and the workers. Bubba Bowers created masterpieces with the arc welder. Coz served as their spiritual adviser and painter. Coz could take a shattered transom and make it whole again with only the sledgehammer and a can of Bondo. A better team of Little Creatures could not be found in all of Freo, perhaps all the world.

The Sausalito 7-Eleven would have done well to follow the Little Creatures to Fremantle. Their diet consisted solely of soda, coffee, salsa, chips, beer, all classic 7-Eleven foods. Why waste time and valuable calories with veggies and fresh fruit? Beer to the Little Creatures was like air to the rest of us.

As the second series drew near, the Little Creatures pace quickened. Swan beer cans, the Aussie equivalent of Strohs, littered their workroom. The big push was on to make the tailor pits smaller. After the tailor pits had shrunk to a more manageable size, Johnno planned to build a complete bathtub unit to make them wholly waterproof. We wanted to race the next series with a full crew of eleven sailors and not ten sailors and one bilge pumper.

31
Round Robin II, Race 1
Barging

Sunday, November 2, 1986, break time was over. The regatta organizers commenced Round Robin II on a weekend, a move that brought cheers from the spectator boat operators. Our race promised to draw the majority of attention from these spectators, the media, and a large portion of the sporting world. Instead of enjoying a few warm-up races against lesser foe, we started Round Robin II against our toughest opponent: Stars and Stripes.

Who could have forgotten that first battle, where we had led around the whole course, right up until the last twenty-five yards, only to lose by six gruesome seconds? So near a victory was the rowing equivalent of losing a race in the last stroke. The few times that happened in my rowing career I had immediately gone crazy and afterward trained especially hard to destroy that last-stroke devil. Certainly we had learned that we were capable of competing in this rarefied America's Cup atmosphere with the hot-shot syndicates like Kiwi Magic, America II, and most importantly, Stars and Stripes. On this quiet Sunday afternoon, with only ten knots of wind to power the sails, we would have a chance to prove it.

Today the rough-and-tumble language of the first race was missing during the prestart sequence. Instead our crew seemed more relaxed and confident. In general we were less concerned with our opponent and more attuned to making our beast go as fast as possible. I found that encouraging. Russell's frequent outbursts during our first encounter went expressly against the three rules for success I had so carefully followed during the Olympic year. Of the three rules, *Stay humble* was the easiest to follow. But by constantly shouting epithets referring to Conner's girth, lineage and sobriety, the notion of staying humble was shot down in flames. Thank God everyone stayed relatively mute.

The whole race was decided at a single mark rounding: at the reaching mark.

Reaching mark is such a romantic name for a point of sail. It is placed off to the left side of the course almost to the out-of-bounds line. Depending on the wind direction, a skipper may call for a reaching spinnaker, or perhaps he will use the jib. With either sail, a 12-meter always makes its best speed to and from the reaching mark.

Approaching the reaching mark, we had chomped into Conner's lead and nipped at his stern until the Stars and Stripes grinders were glancing over their shoulders to see how close we were ranging. It is difficult to pass an opponent at the reaching mark. It is difficult to do anything except watch our bowman, Scott Inveen, slam the after guy into the spinnaker pole as we jibed around the mark. Our desperate need was to be overlapped with their slate-blue hull by the time we entered an imaginary circle extending two boat lengths around the wing mark. If we were overlapped, then Conner would have to give us room to round the mark. This is called *barging room*, as in 'Hate to barge in on you folks, but I'm in a hurry to get back to the dock.'

As we approached the wing mark, Cayard suddenly sprinted towards the bow. He triple-jumped over the pitman, the open hatch, the bowman, until he was alone on the very bow, looking intently toward the stern of the Stars and Stripes.

"Overlap," he screamed. "We have overlap."

With overlap, we were safe for a moment. Conner had to give us room to round the mark since our bow had overlapped their stern. If they had been ahead of our bow, the race might have taken a completely different twist. But with Cayard on the bow yelling the overlapping facts for all to hear, Conner was obliged to give us room around the mark.

The fun wasn't over yet. Immediately after rounding the reaching mark, Conner cranked his wheel hard to port and drove his bow to within inches of the USA stern. This tactic is standard in yacht racing, and if we had been in a similar position Blacky we would have done the same. If Conner tapped us, we would have been disqualified unless we were far enough ahead to claim *mast abeam*. Blacky was right on top of things, and he let Conner know in his classic verbal style that we had *mast abeam* and therefore the right of way.

When the USA finally, jubilantly, crossed the finish line thirty-nine seconds ahead of Stars and Stripes, a red protest flag still flew from Conner's backstay. Ten hours later, the regatta jury phoned Ziggy's Pizza Parlor to supplement their energies. A good meaty protest needed long hours of discussion, especially when the principal characters were such intense competitors. If the jury had as good a vantage point as Blacky and Cayard, then the protest would no doubt be ignored and the victory awarded to the USA.

Somewhere between the time I went to sleep and the dawn, the jury decreed we had won. Victory to the USA over Stars and Stripes.

32
Round Robin II, Race 2
Eagle

Hmmm. Cheese bread. Cheese bread is a slice of plain white bread with thick cheddar cheese grilled on one side. Our new cook, English-born Catherine, celebrated our having beaten Dennis Conner by serving her cheese bread specialty. I loved her for it. She was a classy woman on an around-the-world adventure.

Into my second course, I noticed a persistent rattling of windows that kept me from concentrating on my Rice Bubbles, the Aussie name for Rice Crispies. I looked outside and saw a flock of parrots bolting tail-first past the window. At 7:45 a.m. the wind was already blowing twenty-five knots. Fortunately, we were only racing the Eagle from Newport Beach.

Naturally we claimed to be experts in heavy wind sailing, having survived those wild outings off San Francisco's violent Potato Patch. Today the Eagle-lowlanders would die from fright, except perhaps their massive grinders, Hal and Al, who had played professional football. They had enormous, bloated arms. In Russell's words, "Hal and Al are big citizens."

The Eagle would need more than two legendary pairs of muscle-bound arms to beat the pride of windy San Francisco.

As we drove to the compound after breakfast, navigator and on-board weatherman Craig Healy said, "According to the marine weather service, the wind is going to lessen throughout the day."

He was so wrong we almost threw him overboard halfway around the course. And when it was all over and we were driving back to the crew house, tired and hurting and covered from head to toe with a thin salt glaze, bowman Scott Inveen remarked that the day could be described in only one word: knarly. Scott was right.

From the starting gun, actually from tow out of the harbor, the wind howled through the rigging with such awesome abandon that merely staging a race under such conditions bordered on crazy. The wind was blowing twenty-eight knots at the start, and a minute after we crossed the line a dark squall rolled down the course like a careening freight train. When the squall finally settled on top of us, the sensation was like sailing in a pitch-black wind tunnel.

For the first time since I'd been sailing with him, Blackaller said, "Okay, guys, don't worry about the other boat. Just hang on and keep your head down."

His usual bravado had disappeared, and instead only two things preoccupied his thoughts: keeping our beast afloat and the mast upright. I kept thinking of all those little modifications we had made to the mast and rigging during the last break to make it lighter and more aerodynamic. In the next twenty minutes the force of this squall would test an equally important feature — breaking limit.

The *apparent wind* (true wind plus the speed of the boat into the wind) jumped to forty-five knots as wave after wave tumbled over the bow. Pure white water by the truckload, one wave every three seconds, completely swamped the cockpit. I hoped Healy or Cayard had turned on the electric bilge pump, which is against every yacht racing rule except the one that says it's stupid to sink. The wind shifted so radically during the squall, an unprecedented 110 degrees, that the whole team suddenly became navigators, looking for the windward mark. We found the mark and rounded thirty seconds behind Eagle. Then the fun began. Not many 12s can top the USA for downwind speed, and today we had all the wind we needed to make our beast fly down the waves.

Because of the new wind direction, we didn't hoist the spinnaker for the second leg, running instead with the jib and mainsail only. Now we had our sailing act together like I had never experienced. We were behind Eagle by a hundred yards, and as we gathered speed, the latent surfers in the crew suddenly awakened. We began grinding down the opposition by riding the swells that we had pounded into only minutes before. We picked up momentum in bundles, speed building hard and fast and clean. We had plenty of power, and the waves seemed to take a liking to us. We were eleven men on a sixty-six foot, 66,000-pound surfboard, riding the best waves the Indian Ocean had to offer on this violent summer day. The feeling was intoxicating.

Everyone worked the grinder handles: Healy on aft main sheet handles; Big Mike Erlin and Jim Whitmore on mid-main sheet handles; Hank, Scott Inveen, and I on jib sheet handles, with Sheik cranking the bilge pump handle. We worked in unison like a demented punk rock band playing to an underwater audience, playing for ourselves.

The spectator fleet was locked safe and cozy in the harbor. The ocean belonged to the racers today. Blacky had given the wheel over to Cayard, and when I glanced around I saw Cayard leaning into the swells, cranking bottom turns, working back up the face. We were flat out surfing.

The Eagle was just ahead, and with each wave we drew closer until we needed only one good wave to move past them. The wave we wanted was spawned somewhere off Antarctica, and it came to us full force. Stevie saw it first, and as the wave drew close to our transom he yelled to his waiting grinders: "Trim main. Big gainer on the way. Go for it!"

Healy, Mike, and Whitmore spun their main sheet handles with every ounce of strength, and then the jib grinders took over, tugging the jib closer, gathering just enough acceleration to push us over the top and lock the USA into a deep-green, fifteen-foot wave. As we dropped in, the spray shot off the gunnels, pelting our dry suits like marbles. Each crewman let loose screams of exquisite, uninhibited pleasure. It felt so fine and fast, as though we were sailing right over Niagara Falls.

The speedometer topped fourteen knots, an amazing number considering these boats rarely go over ten knots, and naturally we yelled for more. Our beautiful wave didn't disappoint us. One last nudge pushed us into the rare fifteen-knot range. Our screaming crested then and there. It felt so good to be flying down the face of that wave, surfing our aluminum beast. We passed the Eagle, but that wasn't the issue. We were taking this violent day and loving it, working with it. Just being a part of it was a fantastic honor.

But the day was long from over. After paying a short visit to the reaching mark, we prepared to round the leeward mark for the next to last time. The staysail was down, and the jib was working its way up the headstay. Suddenly the big brother of the wave we had ridden earlier washed across the deck. Inveen, perched on the very tip of the bow, was completely buried in white water; Sheik was flung to the very edge of the boat. Both crewmen struggled to hold the jib, but both had to let go or else be swept overboard. Our beautiful #5 jib was instantly transformed into a sea anchor, and we spent our hard-earned lead gathering it back on deck. Eagle scooted by and we could do nothing but tend to our own fire drill.

At the Newport Harbor Yacht Club and the St. Francis Yacht Clubs it will long be debated whether we should have cut the lines that held the #5 jib, thereby freeing us from our impromptu sea anchor. Or should we haul it back on board? My unsolicited opinion was that we should have cut the lines as though Jaws himself was on the other end.

I tore the wire cutters from the grinding pedestal and held them poised over the port jib wire, waiting for the command to cut us free. Blacky never gave the order to cut the wire.

We needed five long minutes of frantic scrambling to reclaim the jib. By the time we started moving we were too far behind to catch Eagle. Those desperately needed five points went to the lowlanders from Newport Beach, California.

The loss was disappointing, but the worst was yet to come. For the remainder of the regatta, whenever a shortage of points became even a vague topic of conversation, Blackaller threw the Eagle accident and its accompanying loss of five points in our faces with embarrassing consistency.

33
Round Robin II, Race 9
Football, American style

The basement of Fremantle's favorite sailor bar, the Norfolk Tavern, was packed this evening with crewmen from five different American syndicates watching Monday Night Football: St. Louis vs. Washington.

For the first time, I witnessed what happens when someone decides that the game of American football is too long. This version was boxed up tight and clean, with all the time-outs, commercials and interruptions edited from the show. It moves pretty quickly.

Seeing twenty-two guys bouncing into each other on a big-screen television took on the trappings of a peculiar dance, as foreign to the Fremantle natives as their beloved rugby was to me. It didn't matter who was playing or the score or even what quarter we were watching—just enjoying the act of football being played brought us tons of pleasure. Crewmen talked about their favorite team back home: Chicago, New York, San Diego, San Francisco. Then they talked of home. Any animosity that may have existed among competing syndicates was left at the door (or at least on the floor after a few beers). Good times in Freo.

Two days ago we had wind by the busload, and today we had none, or almost none. How could this huge bathtub be so rough-and-tumble one day and so calm the next? The Fremantle Doctor must have taken a few days off to go fishing, or perhaps he simply blew himself out. This patch of Indian Ocean was so calm I could have rowed my single scull to the starting line.

Racing under these conditions was like ghosting over the water, gliding smoothly, no crashing or frantic grabs for handholds. The watchword was control. More damage could be done to the sails by cranking the grinder handles too hard than if a nice steady pressure was applied. The overall sensation was like playing chess after a glass of wine. A big glass. The wind was doled out in tiny amounts, and a boat could jump ahead with a little puff and then sit on the other boat all afternoon.

Most of the day's work involved transferring sails from the Sourdough to the Rubber Duck to the USA. Cayard kept juggling sails back and forth. He was certain a huge blow was only moments away, but it never materialized. The only factor that prevented Cayard from shuffling our whole sail inventory was the fifteen-minute gun. Once it fired he was stuck with the sails he had on board.

On November 11, two days after my thirty-second birthday, we raced the New Zealand 12-meter, Kiwi Magic, KZ7. The start was postponed two-and-a-half hours, and eventually the course was shortened from eight legs to only three.

New Zealand was pretty good. They seemed to have it figured out, *it* being everything 12-meter. New Zealand had demonstrated its excellence by winning twenty-one of twenty-two races with a wicked-fast fiberglass boat, the only 12-meter in Fremantle not made of aluminum. If they could maintain this mad streak, every boat at the next America's Cup would be made of fiberglass, Kevlar, carbon fiber, crepe paper—anything but aluminum.

Okay, so their boat was fast. They also had sails like God would create if he had the time. Stowed in some forty-foot container were a hundred new sails just dying to get out of the bag and fly like gossamer silk. Boat and sails. What's left? Crew. They had a dedicated crew who had been training together for over a year. And their twenty-five-year-old skipper, Chris Dickson, derived an intense pleasure from terrorizing the older men who drove most of the other 12s.

New Zealand would be a tough act to beat, and this afternoon we did little to raise their collective heart rates. With the shortened course we knew the start would be critical, yet we handed it to them without a fight and trailed the rest of the race. Not much fun. Maybe we could challenge them to a friendly game of American football during the next break and take some of the wind out of their sails.

Two days later we ended Round Robin II with resounding victories against Challenge France and our old sparring partner, Chicago's Heart of America. With our beast securely locked into the safety pen we adjourned to the crew house for a barbecue and to drink copious amounts of native beer. (Victoria Bitter my new favorite.) Unfortunately we had little to celebrate relative to our overall standing. Now we were tied with White Crusader for fifth place. Ouch. Even worse, our neighbor French Kiss had leapfrogged over us into a tie with Stars and Stripes for fourth place. No worries, Mate, our little fraternity never let those details stand in the way of a good barbecue.

New Zealand (sixty-six points) had a stranglehold on first place. They sailed an undefeated second series and had tasted defeat only once, against Conner in Round Robin I. America II (fifty-six points) maintained a firm hold on second place; Stars and Stripes (forty-six points) was third; French Kiss (forty-five points) was fourth. Our beast and White Crusader both owned forty-three points.

Blacky attended the barbecue with Christine, although he spent most of the evening by himself in a corner, adding those misplaced Eagle points to our forty-three point total. "We'd be in third place," he mumbled a thousand times over, "if that jib hadn't gone overboard."

34
Blackaller, the man

Break II. Summertime in Fremantle, and the living was easy. We had one day off, worked three days, and then went sailing. But one essential member of the royal *we*, our fearless leader, was conspicuously absent from the fun.

Where could he be? I was worried about him. He didn't tell anyone where he was going. Maybe he'd been kidnapped by his teenage ex-girlfriend and was being tortured at this very moment. He had disappeared once before only to turn up a week later, saying, "Shit, what a fucking joke. That guy in charge at the Australian Grand Prix wouldn't let me drive in the celebrity race. Said he'd never hear of me. I didn't want to race anyway."

This time we had a sneaking suspicion that Blacky had eloped with Christine. Naturally Paul Cayard, a former boyfriend of Christine, made a few predictably jokes. That sort of locker room talk no doubt persuaded Blacky to keep his marriage plans a better secret than the dimensions of our keel. Two knot-tying locations were suspected: Margaret River, a two-hour drive south, and Bali, a four-hour flight north. We never knew where the deed was done.

A hundred years ago Blacky would have been a pirate named Greyhead, spending his days ravaging the Seven Seas, match-racing the Queen's fastest vessels and meeting women the easy way. Now he joked about spending countless months racing a sailboat that went only ten miles an hour with an oversized beer mug as the first place prize. He wondered aloud what his acquaintance Mario Andretti would say to such a peculiar hobby.

When Tom Blackaller's name appeared on the press conference marquee, the media center was always packed, standing room only. The journalists knew they would finally get the hot and juicy quotes to satisfy their desperate editors. Most of the America's Cup skippers were not particularly outspoken or opinionated. Blacky had been marinating in both those sauces for so long he was physically unable to say anything that was not outspoken or opinionated. As Edwin Moses once said, "There is no such thing as bad press," so I'm sure our noble skipper's flippant remarks somehow worked in our favor.

One classic Blacky statement found its way onto a bumper sticker: "We don't just want the Cup, we want the whole damn island."

A box of these noxious bumper stickers was tossed into one of our containers and when opened in Fremantle the customs officer almost revoked our visas. I hated these un-humble stickers from the first moment, and like a recurring nightmare they popped up everywhere in Freo, on bus benches, bar room walls, Kookaburra's compound door. The message was poorly worded, and Blackaller didn't even make it up. Scott Easom read it somewhere, and told Blacky, who immediately assumed ownership.

More original Blacky quotes wafted thick in the hot summer sun, like the classic line he spouted just as we crossed the starting line against Challenge France in Round Robin I. The wind was howling through the rigging, the crew was hunkered down in anticipation of twenty-four miles of slam-dancing, when suddenly Blacky yelled: "The only fucking way we're going to lose this fucking race is if one of you motherfuckers falls off the fucking boat."

Words to live by.

I fondly remember the recent team meeting (complete with a San Francisco television crew who were visiting Fremantle) where Blacky paced relentlessly in front of the troops, saying, "I won't stand for any more cut tacks. Ya got that? No more cut tacks."

Another good rule to live by, except no one knew what he meant by *cut tack*.

We looked at each other with guarded smiles, unsure if the meeting's mock solemnity would permit a full-fledged laughing seizure. Finally we deciphered the phrase. Blacky was referring to cutting the jib sheet during a tack when a dreaded override was in progress. In all our months of sailing, thousands of tacks, we had endured exactly one cut tack.

I was working in the sail loft when suddenly Blacky screamed down from his office, "Who hired Rick Fleig?"

Rick Fleig, standing right next to me, almost passed out when he heard those words. Rick was a recent graduate of the Courageous school of 12-metering, and he had been an excellent asset to our program since being hired about a month before. When Blacky didn't get an immediate response, he screamed again, "Who the hell hired Rick Fleig?"

Rick was sure he had committed some fatal error and now he was on his way back to New Hampshire. Actually, Blacky needed this vital bit of information to answer a minor bookkeeping question.

Blackaller, the man. He symbolized our fraternity the same way Ronald McDonald carried the mantle for McDonalds. We needed Blacky, if merely for the comic relief. He could be damn funny when the muse struck him.

At dinner one evening we heard some heavy breathing coming from the basement workout room. The rowing machine hummed in a low tone for a short time and then stopped altogether. Blacky stumbled up the steps, red-faced, clutching his heart. He was sweating as though he had just escaped from an overheated sauna. When he caught his breath, he said, "I couldn't take another stroke. Holy shit. That thing is tough. I wanted to go 500 meters, and I only got to 350. Geez, that thing's a bitch."

Bruce Epke and I usually rowed at least 20 kilometers for our workouts. At that point I mostly hoped Blacky would survive the competition. At least once every few minutes Blacky would shout: "I just couldn't take another stroke. Not one more stroke."

I regretted that Blacky was not more obsessed with our project, in the style of Dennis Conner. Blacky was simply not approaching the challenge as though his life depended on it. And that almost guaranteed we would fall short of

157

winning the Cup. Overall, the crew wanted to win, and we were willing to behave in the necessary obsessed manner. But we desperately needed our leader to join in.

This lack of commitment showed most in the lack of time he devoted to on-the-water practice. Our radical front-rudder *canard* called for constant practice under every condition. Yet Blacky refused to make even a moderate effort. Blacky was always race-ready, but anything other than racing drove him to distraction. Blacky was a suitable figurehead for the syndicate, and he cannot be faulted for his fund-raising efforts. As a skipper he was wrong. We needed someone lean and hungry, like Cayard only with more confidence, to pull off this Cup miracle.

A week after Blacky disappeared, a ransom note arrived in the form of an invitation to wedding reception.

I attended the reception, if only to find out where Blacky lived and to glimpse his secretive lifestyle. To my great surprise I discovered he lived in a tired old house with a moldy backyard pool. I wouldn't have guessed it.

35
The Cup, up Close

Toward the end of Break II, we were treated to a special affair. The actual America's Cup, the source of all this madness, excitement, and general aquatic insanity, was finally coming out of the shadows and into the limelight. About time. After all, millions of dollars had been spent to acquire the damn thing. We might as well see what we we're working toward.

The unveiling occasion? I'm not sure why this intimate gathering for 3,500 people was convened. My engraved invitation said bluntly: America's Cup Cocktail Party.

Nice invite, with official-looking lettering. But at the bottom were the worrisome words *jacket and tie*. Some of the humblest thrift stores in Freo were canvassed in a last-minute search for the missing jacket.

At the appointed time our humble band of sailors loaded into the team vans and drove to the Royal Perth Yacht Club, home of Australia II, Alan Bond, boxing kangaroos, winged keels, and, most importantly, the America's Cup. The USA contingent walked arm-in-arm through the yawning gate of the Royal Perth Yacht Club like the proud representatives of San Francisco that we were. A feistier, healthier, thirstier 12-meter crew was not to be seen the whole night. All our friends and family, skeptics and fans back home could rest assured, we looked good.

A huge tent housing the buffet tables was set up between the main clubhouse and the Swan River, and next to the tent a petite orchestra had staked its ground. A strong breeze shook the jacaranda trees and blew purple flowers onto the lawn. The wind added a strange atmosphere, as though something bizarre could happen at any moment. Parties like this are supposed to be held on serene, cloudless nights, but for this occasion the wind was blowing twenty knots true. The nearby boats tied at their moorings rocked back and forth, their halyards slapping in time to a heaven-sent beat.

A weird selection of food graced the buffet table: squab (pigeon) on a stick, buffalo steaks, thin-sliced dugite snake on pita bread, and for dessert, beetroot ice cream. Seconds, anyone? Lots more food. For ladies, the dress of the day was basic anything-goes. One young lady wore only two sequined eye patches between her sternum and clavicle. An ocean of drinks were spilled in her wake.

Minutes after 9:00 p.m. the America's Cup arrived in person. A man spoke into a microphone about the great things that had come to Perth and Fremantle because of the America's Cup, and how they'd really hate to see it go, and how happy he was that we could all make it this evening. And finally, direct from a limited engagement at the New York Yacht Club, the one and only, solid silver, solid tradition, (don't even think about touching it!), 100 Guinea Cup, aka The America's Cup.

For a long moment the lights shut down, and then suddenly a solitary spotlight slashed across the pitch-black night. The light shone clear and clean on a barge set a few yards from the shore. The crowd fell silent as a few tentative threads of dry-ice smoke issued from the barge. The silence was broken by the in-house band's excellent rendition of Men at Work's *We Come from a Land Down Under*. This song became famous as the fight-psych song of Australia II at the last America's Cup, and the whole crowd mouthed the words in time to the music.

The Cup slowly rose like a timid child from the bowels of the barge until its whole grandeur was exposed for our viewing pleasure. The Cup looked cold, all alone on the barge, the wind whistling around its silver girth. For minutes on end the crowd screamed their delight as fireworks shook and jammed overhead. The Cup had arrived.

Our newest teammate, Ricky Fleig, had left his glasses at home, and he wanted a closer look at the Cup. At first this seemed like an impossible dream, but this is Oz, and things happen fast and strange. By chance, Rick met the last living charter member of the Royal Perth Yacht Club, Jed Jenkins. At well past the departing hour, Rick, his girlfriend Connie, and the elderly Mr. and Mrs. Jenkins decided to have a closer look at the Cup. Mr. Jenkins, because of his honored position with the RPYC, had access to the key that unlocked the private trophy room where the Cup had now been transferred for safekeeping.

Mr. Jenkins was also the oldest living recipient of an artificial aorta valve, which made him a tough guy to insure. He was still game, however, and he might have had a little too much champagne to drink. Regardless of the reason, he fumbled with the key and then threw back the trophy room door as though coming home from a hard day at work. The four troopers walked into the trophy room, three steps onto the red carpet, left turn toward the wall, and finally the Cup was exposed for their private feasting. They took one collective step forward, and without warning an alarm screamed to attention.

"Damn that thing," Mr. Jenkins said.

"Easy, dear, remember your heart," his wife reminded.

"Damn my heart. Can't even hear myself."

"Dear, I'll go downstairs and have the guard turn off the alarm. Don't you get excited."

Mrs. Jenkins went back down the steps while Rick, Connie, and Mr. Jenkins walked closer to the glass case. The Cup held center stage, but it wasn't alone in the trophy case. On both sides were the Louis Vuitton Challenger Cup and the Defender Cup, which paled to mere paperweight proportions in the America's Cup shadow.

Connie and Rick bent forward for a closer look, using both hands to shield their ears from the throbbing alarm. The Cup drew them on like a magnet. One last step and their heads were only inches from the case. Connie leaned forward just a tick more, and suddenly, like a hatchet from heaven, a thick steel wall sprang from the ceiling, zoomed a millimeter from Connie's beak, and slammed into the red carpet with a crash.

"Wow, close call, eh, Mr. Jenkins?" Rick said.

But Mr. Jenkins didn't hear. Mr. Jenkins was reeling back against the side wall and grabbing at his pants pocket. He was looking for some nitroglycerin tablets or vitamins or something, which he soon found and stuffed down his throat. Then he limped downstairs, muttering about calling his doctor.

When all was finally straightened out, the alarm turned off, and the seven hundred-pound steel curtain returned to its guillotine position, a tired USA crew piled into the van and went looking for an open McDonalds.

36
Round Robin III, Race 2

Round Robin III, the final round robin, started off with a bang. The mood before our first race could be summed up in one word: tense. With twelve whopping points on the line, the flame under our tails had increased from the simmer of one-point Round Robin I, past the broil of five-point Round Robin II, to full-fledged nuclear meltdown: 12 mammoth points for each victory. Months ago Blacky had made headlines when he said at a press conference that a win in Round Robin I was worth $100,000. How much were they worth now?

In the first race of Round Robin III against Italia that money angle quickly became insignificant. We lost, and that was all that mattered. We had led a big chunk of the race despite stumbling over the starting line early. While rounding the last leeward mark another major disaster occurred: the spinnaker escaped from the starboard hatch, dove underwater, and wrapped around the keel. We never recovered, and with that loss our overall standing slipped to ordinary, middle-of-the-pack status.

Our second race of Round Robin III against Challenge France was more interesting, mainly because the Fremantle Doctor settled in for a long visit. So much water came over the bow I thought I would drown from the sensory overload.

Just before we left the dock, tender captain Mik Beatie looked toward the ocean from his flying bridge and said, "Best get suited up early and dress warm. Looks like all hell's breaking loose out there."

My dry suit was the perfect choice, with a foul-weather jacket on top and polypropylene long johns underneath. This is known as dressing for survival, hooting Indian Ocean style.

"These boats were simply never designed for this much wind," Jim Whitmore said to me as we towed to the starting line. "There's too little freeboard and too many places where the water pours into the sewer on days like today." His words were not the most reassuring to hear as the wind crept towards thirty knots.

The officials said later that if the wind had blown at the start like it did at the end of the race, they would never have started the race. After seeing America II lose two men overboard, and most boats round at least one mark without a jib, or in Azzurra's case without a mainsail, I believe we had finally reached the top limit of race-able wind. On the reaching leg, our wind meter read 35.3 knots, and this was not in a squall—it was simply pure, unadulterated, screaming wind. I clipped an article from the next day's newspaper, which stated this was the windiest America's Cup race day in modern history.

Grinding on super-windy days is like riding a roller coaster for five or six hours: working that fine line between pure fear and soul-cleansing ecstasy. The great white knuckler incarnate, surging over the waves on the upwind legs, crashing down the backsides so hard that it seemed inevitable that something break.

"Steering feels a little mushy," Blacky said after all sixty thousand pounds crested an unusually steep wave and then slammed bow-first into the water. "Timmer, take a look and see if it's still there."

Bowman Dana Timmer scuttled to the bow and leaned over the starboard railing for a second. Then he came back with his damage report.

"Careful next time you tack," Dana said. "The front rudder is busted in half."

Without a front rudder, our tacking ability was questionable—perhaps even nonexistent. We kept sailing to the edge of the race course until we were well past the lay line. Then we slowly tacked for the mark. Stevie and Russ used their respective sails to steer our beast while Blacky held the rudder steady. With our huge lead Cayard had previously decided not to use a spinnaker on the next run. But the broken front rudder quickly changed those plans. We carefully hoisted the spinnaker, and, as we had done with the jib and mainsail on the upwind leg, Hank and Russ trimmed the spinnaker to help steer us to the leeward mark.

The equipment takes a wicked beating when the wind tops thirty knots. An ordinary snap shackle will refuse to open and then abruptly disintegrate under the pressure. But for all this wind, we did not go any faster. The only consistent response was that everything cinched tighter and loaded up and broke, and people were hurt or fell overboard, or a $150,000 front rudder shattered as though run over by a steamroller. We survived and collected our 12 sodden points.

But the day was not over. After the boat had been tucked in for the night we trudged upstairs to Blackaller's office for the tenth meeting since this program began. Only the actual sailing crew, sixteen men in total, were invited into the office. Once inside, we closed the door against the outside world.

Beginning with Round Robin III we had instigated daily team meetings, perhaps something we should have done from the start. So far not one had been dull.

Every sport has its own version of the obligatory team meeting. At the big national team rowing camps I learned to hate these meetings because it usually meant someone was going to get cut from the squad. Often that person was me. But when I trained by myself for the last few years, I had only one-man team meetings that usually convened at local donut shop. At these meetings never a discouraging word was heard.

This evening I took my place on the floor across from Blacky's desk. In the few seconds before the meeting started I glanced at the artwork: pictures of Blacky driving race cars at Daytona, at Sears Point, at Laguna Seca, at Watkins Glen. One picture showed Blacky racing a Star dingy, and another very small picture showed Defender losing to Liberty. A picture of Blackaller standing next to his daughter Lisa neatly symbolized their relationship. They were only inches apart but looking in completely different directions.

The first order of business was to open any available windows and crank up the air-conditioning. Already the room was starting to grow hot. Then Blacky began the meeting with a small bombshell.

"The word filtering back to me from San Francisco," he said, "is that the folks at home think our crew work is sloppy."

Oh, yes. I could see that yesterday's loss to Italia had caused our skipper to lose some sleep last night. Perhaps he had spent the wee hours calculating the monetary ramifications of the defeat. Now he wanted to reclaim that amount in the form of someone's hide. Two hides immediately came to mind: sewerman Bruce *Sheik* Epke and bowman Scott Inveen. Both men had sailed yesterday, and both had been replaced for today's race, although under the normal crew rotation they would have sailed. Blacky had his speech all ready to go, but didn't want to waste it on the wrong audience.

Blacky: Where's Sheik and Inveen?

Cayard: Sheik's at home. Inveen's downstairs.

Blacky: Well, get him up here.

Cayard: No, Chief. You go down there.

Blacky left the office, his face twisted in disgust as though preparing for the most unpleasant task in the known world. If some other way existed for Blacky to exit the building, I'm sure he would have made use of it. A minute later both Blacky and Inveen walked into the office.

Inveen, suddenly, catching Blacky off guard: Did you say that Sheik and I were never to sail again?

Blacky: No, I never said that.

Inveen: Look me straight in the eye and say that.

Blacky: No. You're mistaken. I never said that.

Inveen: You're a lying sack of shit.

The secretary in the outer office rolled another sheet of paper into her typewriter and pretended not to have heard. The fan on the air conditioner slowed as though for an instant the power had been turned off. Inveen's word rambled around the room like lazy ghosts, finally perching on Blacky's shoulders.

We sat still and waited for something to happen. Inveen may have been crying. Blacky could not decide what to do. Had Blacky said that Inveen and Sheik would never sail again? If not, he could have thrown Inveen out the window. He had the right, but only if he wasn't lying. I knew the truth. Everyone knew. Blackaller was lying. Blackaller said nothing.

Fellow grinder Jeff Littfin: The whole management of this syndicate has been awful. Speaking for myself, I'm disgusted with the whole program.

Blacky: I've been busy raising money. Eight million dollars.

Whitmore: I've never seen worse foredeck work in my whole life. But the problems are coming from the back of the boat. You're simply not giving us enough time leading into maneuvers.

Blacky: I could have my wife on the boat if I wanted. I run this show.

Whitmore: How could you not know about the J-locks?

(J-locks are small shackles that hook the jib sheet to the jib. The foredeck needs to know how the skipper plans to approach the mark, floater drop or standard leeward takedown, for example, before they can hook up the essential J-locks in the correct orientation. I had learned the necessity of the foredeck knowing this information after my second day of sailing. In yesterday's meeting Blacky had claimed not to know the importance of telling the foredeck which type of drop he planned on using.)

Blacky: Maybe I could have said those things about Sheik and Inveen. I was so pissed off yesterday I couldn't see straight. But I'm much more aware of what's going on than you fuckers know. Do you think I go home and sleep? My time is better spent thinking than wet-sanding the boat.

Jeff Littfin: This is not a team. Only a group of individuals. Our team spirit is missing.

Whitmore: How could you sail so long and not know the J-locks had to come off?

Blacky: My watch stopped. My damn watch stopped before the start of the Italia race. That's why we went over early.

Scott Inveen was a good bowman, but unfortunately for him we had another, equally good bowman in Dana Timmer. Sheik was a different story. Sheik's sewerman ability was superb. He never gave up. He was the captain of the crew. He had invited me into this little fraternity. Blacky should never have blamed Sheik or Inveen for his failings. Sheik didn't pout. He would simply quit if he were not to sail again. Although we had enough crew to fill his vacancy, we had no one to replace Sheik's spirit. I marveled at the ignorance of our skipper.

Poor Blacky. He raised the money, but he forgot what the money was for. He forgot to practice. He forgot to give us respect. He sailed all those months, but he was not paying attention. He didn't know the basic element of leeward mark roundings. You fucked up, Blacky. You ignored the main tenet of my three Olympic gold medal rules: Take complete responsibility for the outcome of the race. Instead you chose the path to certain failure by blaming someone else, the foredeck in this instance.

After Blacky cooled off a few days later, Inveen sailed only one more race. Sheik sailed on a regular basis. I doubted if Sheik or Inveen would sail the next Cup with Tom Blackaller.

The day after the big meeting we raced and easily defeated Azzurra, exactly as we had done in the first two round robins. We still had a slim chance of claiming a spot in the final four if we could defeat our lesser opponents, such as Heart of America. The Heart wouldn't put up much fight, or so we thought.

37
Unzipped
Round Robin III, Race 4

Buddy Melges, wonderfully nicknamed *Muddy Bilges*, is a true sailing character. He always sailed with one hand in his pocket, even in the worst gale. The whole Indian Ocean could have been crashing down on him, yet Buddy would still look bemused, slightly bored or pleasantly sanguine. He drove his 12-meter with the nonchalance of a man on a merry-go-round. On this early December day we raced Buddy.

He had done some amazing things to his craft during the last break, and lo and behold, he had a contender. During the break his crew, including Buddy in person, not just in spirit, worked day and night, adding *tiplets* onto their wings. Now when the Heart heeled over in a strong breeze, the wings nearly protruded through the surface.

Buddy was fond of saying, "We don't tack anymore. We bank-turn like an F-14."

He had beaten America II a few days earlier, which had served as a warning to all the challengers that the Heart of America was a tough, new 12-meter force to be taken seriously on Gage Roads. No longer was the Heart inexorably linked to the bottom dwellers like Challenge France and Azzurra.

After a promising start we held the lead for the first two legs of the race. Just as we were about to drop the spinnaker and turn upwind we had a rare *zipper blowout*.

A fragile zipper might seem out of place on a 12-meter, but every boat had them, including two on the mainsail. For downwind sailing we could benefit from more sail area. Extra sail footage was hidden in two places: at the foot of the mainsail (parallel to the boom) and along the luff of the mainsail, (parallel to the mast). The only way to access this extra square-footage was by releasing the zipper that ran the length of the foot and the zipper that ran the length of the luff. (When the wind was hooting, the zippers stayed shut.)

Today both zippers opened fine for the downwind run, but when Stevie, our zipper expert, went to re-zip toward the end of the run, the zipper along the mast became stuck and would not budge. Instant disaster.

We turned upwind with the extra hunk of sail flapping in the wind—needless to say, a very slow sail shape. Ten minutes later the Heart went past and assumed an oppressive position, sitting on our beast like a sumo wrestler. We were never able to recapture the lead, and those twelve invaluable points vanished into the depths.

We had finally come full circle. My first day in San Francisco we had sailed and lost to Buddy's Heart of America, and now, on this near last day in Fremantle, again we'd been defeated by the *Wizard of Zenda*.

Despite the fact that his success came at our expense, I was extremely happy for Buddy and his crew. Buddy had proved himself to be a first-class competitor and in general an extremely good guy. His team was passionately devoted to him, and I doubt if a closer knit crew could have been found in all of Fremantle.

If we had not lost today we would have been sharing fourth place with White Crusader. Our next opponent would be Crusader, and that would sort out the mess. Whoever lost would not make the semi-finals.

38
Round Robin III, Race 5
0:00:03:

Eagle had landed, permanently. Some gremlin with an adding machine figured out the Eagle was already numerically eliminated from the final four. The same little gremlin gave us the frightening news that we could lose only one more race and avoid a similar fate. Today's race was especially important because our opponent, White Crusader, owned exactly twelve points more than we did. If they won, we would have been in such a deep hole that we might never have climb out.

The match was set for 1:40 p.m., Green Course, fifteen knots of breeze.

Just as the crews were toweling off before the first bell a strange thing occurred. In the race before our battle, America II versus Italia, both boats went over the starting line early. For the first time in this regatta a *general recall* flag was hoisted from the committee boat. In the immortal words of navigator Craig Healy, "No big deal."

Unfortunately, this little inconvenience turned into a big bummer soon after our start. The first race on our course, French Kiss versus New Zealand, was in the midst of a close battle. They rounded the leeward mark just as we began sailing up the course for the first time. The confusing end result was that instead of a simple match race, we had to take on the Kiwis and French Kiss and White Crusader at the same time, a virtual fleet race. The feeling was like trying to play two concurrent baseball games on the same diamond. Boats kept jostling into each other, tacking to stay clear, until finally a giant knot formed as we approached the first mark rounding. Like a Christmas shopping frenzy, all four boats lunged at the bright orange Louis Vuitton marker buoy at the same time. We came out empty-handed, bruised, and annoyed while White Crusader powered ahead to a 46 second lead.

Their lead shrank on the downwind leg, grew again upwind, teetered on the reaching leg. We were getting closer, but the race was quickly drawing toward the finish. On the last downwind leg we closed the gap to only nine seconds, nine puny seconds, but Crusader had proved to be faster on the upwind legs all afternoon. The time had come to dig deep into our match racing bag of tricks.

With a length to the last mark Blackaller screamed, "Trip the chute," and like a sewerman's nightmare our spinnaker collapsed into the water instead of down the hatch. For a long second everyone thought we were going to have another spinnaker overboard disaster of the Italia variety. From beneath decks the wild cursing of sewerman

Whitmore (Sheik's temporary replacement) shook the whole boat is he frantically tried to pull the spinnaker down the hatch. Finally he found the right handle, and the chute was reclaimed. We rounded the mark inside of White Crusader, whose crew was having also having trouble taming its spinnaker.

Seconds after rounding the mark, Crusader tacked without getting up to speed, and that put it in a very bad position. We bore off a little and then started *hauling the mail* as Russ Silvestri likes to say, for the right side of the course. When both boats came back together a minute later, the USA had a two-length lead. The right side of the course was favored, and White Crusader had given it to us like an early Christmas present. Twenty tacks later we crossed the finish line with the slimmest lead of exactly 0:00:03—three puny seconds.

No big deal.

But the Brits' peevish little skipper, Harold Cudmore, was not through. A small red handkerchief streamed from White Crusader's backstay, the demon protest flag. We had protested only once—Blacky disliked protesting because the jury kept him away from his bride and the bar. The Brits, however, loved to protest, or at least their skipper had a taste for the red flag. Only the White Crusader syndicate had protested the late arrival of Challenge France back in September. That was only the beginning.

Today's protest was equally bizarre: they claimed that our chase boat had ranged too close to the competing 12-meters. A more trivial bone of contention could not be found in all yacht racing. The most annoying part of their protest was that they were right. Rubber Duck Captain

Hogan Beatie was, in fact, closer than the 200-yard minimum distance that the regatta rules allowed. Hogan did not interfere with either of the two 12-meters, but the jury, with a strict rule interpretation, could still dock our twelve points. Hogan hung his head through dinner. His bags were packed and waiting by the back door in case he should be found guilty.

The final verdict arrived by phone. The protest was upheld, but instead of deducting points, a formal reprimand was issued to Hogan. Our team still had a shot at making the semi-finals.

39
Round Robin III, Race 6
Blacky vs. Connor

Today we put on our bulletproof Kevlar vests and went hunting for Conner. Or was he hunting us? Either way, the time had come to boogie.

A black summer rain cloud sat on Fremantle that morning, and that usually meant the wind would be light. The flag on the transom barely shifted as we towed out of the harbor to the race course. Our lightest mainsail, the #10, seemed like the perfect call. So perfect, in fact, that it was already battened and flaked on the boom. Conner hated light wind and reveled in the heavy stuff, the nasty wind this place is renowned for. So far, on December 8, Day of Infamy Part II, the breaks were coming our way.

To our dismay, the black cloud departed an hour later and left us with a clear blue sky that stretched to Antarctica and back. On the flip side, it picked up a load of wind, and the #10 main suddenly became obsolete. The #20 main was now the right sail. But just as it plopped on the deck, the wind jumped another notch. Now the #30 was appropriate.

Dennis Conner had found his wind, his prayers were answered, and our huge, ex-football-playing grinder, Mike Erlin, tied his shoes for the third time.

Mike was the perfect heavy-weather grinder: fearless, incredibly strong, and a good swimmer just in case he should fall overboard. Our whole gang of grinders: Odd-job, Jeff Littfin, Mike Erlin, and I, had seen plenty of sailing in the Cup. We liked each other, and best of all, we were not afraid to shout out some good old-fashioned cheers of encouragement. That elusive team spirit seemed to strive within our clique. That spirit would be needed today among the whole crew.

Nervous is not the right word to describe the feeling on board as Blacky swung the bow toward the starting line. Frantic hysteria, still falls short. Just before Blacky dipped the line, Mike tied his shoes again. This was it.

A few thousand semi-seasick spectators licked their lips in anticipation of the start. A heavy clash was predicted, maybe even a real-life fight between Blacky and Conner. Winch handles would certainly be flying. A dozen press helicopters hovered above the line like bees outside the hive.

Blacky dug deep into his match racing playbook for a different sort of starting technique. To everyone's surprise, he trotted out the classic *Amy Vanderbilt*.

Like a time-tested chess opening, the Amy Vanderbilt has been around since Thomas Lipton was a pup. It works something like this: at the ten-minute gun, the skipper employing the *Amy* turns his boat directly away from the competition and heads for the hills. Adios, Stars and Stripes. See you in a few minutes, maybe. We were gone.

"It sure saves a lot of wear and tear on the equipment," Blacky said later.

With exactly five-and-a-half minutes until the starting gun, Blacky spun the wheel and we headed full steam back towards the starting line. Amy Vanderbilt was smiling, and Dennis Connor was left without a way to counterattack. Gone were the usual circling, sparring, and jousting maneuvers before the start. We captured the favored side of the line, and Conner fell in behind as we crossed three seconds ahead.

On this first tack Stars and Stripes lived a long time in the same relative position: a little behind and a little below us. Conner couldn't point higher, and he couldn't go faster. He was stuck. The minutes ticked by, and he didn't scoot past. Conner was human after all. The mood on our boat took a noticeable turn about that time. The anxiety masks tilted upward and then came off altogether. Our uptight crew began to relax a little bit. Yes, we belonged here. Maybe we were good enough to beat Conner in twenty-six knots of breeze. Why the heck not?

No reason in the world why not. We stretched our lead to the first mark, held it, and even built on the margin throughout the race. We played a conservative game all day, covering Dennis when necessary, taking the wind shifts that looked like they'd stick around for more than ten seconds.

Toward the end of the race, the last and final beat, Mike Erlin tied his shoes for the tenth time that afternoon and then hunkered down for the inevitable tacking duel. Everyone figured that Conner would throw tacks our way like rice at a wedding. Surprisingly the duel never materialized. Eight puny tacks on the last beat, and the USA crossed the finish line forty-two seconds ahead. The beer flowed like water when we returned to the dock.

Twelve more points were added to our total. Now things were getting interesting. The next day we would race Canada II and then Eagle. If we won those races, this interminable war would be distilled into the final three races against America II, French Kiss, and Kiwi Magic.

Everyone had a warm feeling after today's race. Three times we'd battled Conner, coming away with two victories and one very close loss. If we survived the next five races, I thought we might do well in the semi-finals.

40
Round Robin III, Race 9

The writing was spray-painted in neon colors on the bathroom wall:
December 13
USA versus America II
Sink or semi-finals.

In Race 7 we left Canada II high and dry. In Race 8 the Eagle, aka the *Friendly Beagle*, rolled over and played dead. Those had been fun races. Now a place in the semi-finals was tantalizingly close. A win and we'd still be in the hunt. A loss and adios.

Naturally the preparations were extra-special. For starters, we wet-sanded the boat, but not any ordinary wet sanding. This morning for the first time, Kenny Keefe brought out a small, case like a fancy jewel box, and under the protective cover of our safety pen he unsnapped the lid. We privileged few, who had somehow earned this morning's wet-sanding detail, feasted on the contents like starving dogs: 1,200-grit wet/dry sandpaper. Our clumsy hands trembled to be holding such a fine grit—until now most of us had never seen anything finer than 600-grit. This new stuff was intoxicating beyond description. Kenny had smuggled the 1,200-grit into the country way back in August, hoarding his stash until the right time, this very moment. An hour later our keel, the Geek, shone and blushed under our caressing hands. This magnificent aquatic beast was ready for battle.

At 10:30 a.m., with preparations complete, a few final words of encouragement passed between friends and crew. Blackaller's dad had the last say as the USA eased out of the safety pen: "Good luck, Tommy."

"Thanks, Dad."

Those were the last words, more or less, that Blacky spoke until 5:06 p.m., Western Oz time. The cone of silence was now in effect. Not since we had trained in San Francisco had the fabled *cone of silence* been dropped on our humble crew. We hadn't practiced the cone since leaving home, but no one could forget the concept: banishing all talking on the boat, forcing the captain and crew to anticipate each maneuver. Instead of our usual yelling, cursing, and uptight state of mind, every action was to be performed with extra caution and finesse. The grinders loved the cone of silence, since we had nothing to say anyway.

Moments before the start, with the now mute Blacky twisted up tighter than a rodeo bull, the race committee hoisted the race postponement flag. Ouch. When that little red-and-white striped triangle showed above the committee boat, the sails automatically came down and a whole new wardrobe was recruited from the Sourdough. A heavier mainsail was signaled for, the old one dropped, the battens removed, and bagged. Then the new one was made ready and hoisted. Total time: about eight minutes. This was a nice bit of crew work and a good pre-race warm-up. The cone of silence was stressed a bit during the sail change, but mostly it held shape.

During this short break I wondered what thoughts might be rattling the skulls of the opposing America II grinders. The big-money, New York Yacht Club supporters were peering down from their multimillion-dollar luxury yacht, perhaps on the phone at this very second making a reservation for the whole crew to ride home on a fetid sheep ship. America II's failure to make the semi-finals would serve as the ultimate indignation for this dedicated team. I didn't envy them.

More than any other syndicate, the money Gods ruled the America II show, and lately the Gods had been angry. A quick notice of their heavy-handed approach to winning the Cup is needed to put it all in perspective: the America II show had been here forever—three long years of training in Fremantle. Most of the crew had forsaken their Bronx accents for Paul Hogan brogues. During the last break an American II crewman married the cook of the South Australia syndicate. America II had three 12-meters, a virtual quiver of 12s to choose from. They had the heaviest of sponsors—Newsweek, Amway, Cadillac—and a few silent contributors who could buy Western Australia and ship it to Texas should the muse strike them. One or two tiny things had escaped America IIs meticulous preparation. For instance, the San Francisco Eleven and the Geek.

Finally the fifteen-minute gun sounded, and the USA was more or less ready. Today's starting tactic was again our patented *Amy Vanderbilt*. On the flip side, heading back toward the starting line, we had excellent position on America II. With a minute until the start Blacky turned the boat into the wind to luff the sails and slow our progress to the line. America II was about fifteen feet to starboard, and they luffed right with us. A few moments into the luffing session it became clear that America II, which had the right-of-way because of its slightly leeward position, was trying like crazy to hit our boat. Any contact—even a gentle love tap with their jibsail—would cause us to forfeit the race. Blacky played it semi-cool and kept us just out of their reach. We crossed the starting line with a three-second lead and with America II boxed nicely against the committee boat. Unfortunately, both boats were over the starting line early, and as the rules dictate, we had to circle around and clear ourselves by sailing underneath the line.

But the first time we tried to clear ourselves we fell short by about ten feet. We had to do it again. That was a disaster. After our second attempt, the race committee dropped the *over early* placard and we were free to enter the race course. America II needed only one attempt to clear herself, and the end result showed us spotting her a twenty-eight-second lead. No worries, mate.

The cone of silence was still in effect, thus preventing a screaming match between Russ and his least favorite person, America II's tactician, John Bertrand. Everyone stayed quiet, all funneling their energy into a white-hot concentration to trim the sails and make the USA fly through the water. Today the USA—boat and crew—was in the groove.

On the first downwind leg Blacky put on his turn indicator, waited for a safe passing lane, and then scooted around the America II as though they were Sunday sightseers. That, in a nutshell, was that—muted, controlled, flawless crew work and 1,200-grit sandpaper did the trick. Our winning margin was: 2:17.

For the first time in this round robin, we had entered the top four. Tomorrow we could make it stick by beating French Kiss. I volunteered for the morning wet-sanding session.

41
Round Robin III, Race 10

To be finally, completely assured a place in the semifinals we needed to beat French Kiss. Equally important, New Zealand's Kiwi Magic had to defeat America II. If those two independent, non-intersecting events took place, all the time, money, and sweat welded into this campaign would be worthwhile.

But what if New Zealand wanted to race America II instead of us in the semi-finals? They could easily miss a few crucial wind shifts and let America II stroll away with the victory. Blacky stayed up all night devising a way of making sure New Zealand sailed with their usual warriorlike attitude. Blacky's solution was to bet New Zealand that they would defeat America II. Blacky offered this wager at the press conference: if Kiwi Magic defeated America II, Blacky would pay $5,000. Conversely, if New Zealand lost, Blacky would be paid the same amount.

Before we could worry about New Zealand, however, we had to worry about French Kiss. Like Stars and Stripes, their beast performed best in heavy wind. But to their disadvantage, the Fremantle Doctor had been on Christmas vacation of late. Even an hour's delay by the race committee couldn't conjure up a big breeze, so the races were started with only ten slim knots rippling the water. After two endless legs, French Kiss had a ten-second lead coming into the first leeward mark.

"Looks like they're sleeping over there," Russ said as Blacky closed in for the kill. The French were definitely taking an extended break approaching the leeward mark, as though they couldn't imagine a crew so ill-mannered as to nudge ahead in the last few moments before the rounding. Blacky nudged, and we never looked back.

On the last beat, with French Kiss firmly in the bag, all eyes on our boat, from Blacky to bowman Timmer, were focused on the New Zealand vs. America II battle. As the USA crossed the line exactly 1:52 ahead of French Kiss, the question was immediately put to Blacky: "Do you want to stay and watch the outcome or head back to the harbor?" Blacky paused for a second, thinking perhaps of the $5,000 that was riding on the outcome, not to mention the $8 million that was bobbing underneath in the form of our own beast.

"Yeah," he said, "we've got a few minutes to kill. Why not?"

The wind had dropped to a whisper by this time, excellent power-tanning weather, and the USA joined the two hundred spectator boats to witness the outcome.

Would the New York Yacht Club /America II bludgeon approach to winning the America's Cup pull them through? Certainly 132 years of holding the Cup must count for something. Would the Kiwis play straight arrow or twist our collective heads in a vise? The boats stayed close right to the finish, so close that no one could predict the outcome. With one last gasp, Kiwi Magic slid across the finish line with the barest six-second lead. Long live the Kiwis.

We were in. Regardless of the outcome of tomorrow's final race, the top four standings were set in stone.

But what about the $5,000 wager that Blacky now owed? Blacky's response at that evening's press conference was simple: his bet had never been accepted by Michael Fay, the New Zealand syndicate's leader. He gave their skipper, Chris Dickson, a token interest payment of $12 and declined a double-or-nothing bet on tomorrow's race: USA against Kiwi Magic.

Thirteen Challengers had shown up in October to test their skills and boat speed. Some brought two boats or even three. Thirteen optimistic crews proudly wore their team gear around Fremantle like blessed young soldiers fighting a decent, civilized war. The opposing armies met at the Norfolk Tavern for a beer in the evening and then cursed each other the next day on the aquatic battlefield off Fremantle. For the majority of sailors this strange, satisfying, sweet life was over. Only four challengers were left: Kiwi

Magic, French Kiss, Stars and Stripes, and the USA. The rest would be home for Christmas.

42

Round Robin III, the final race

I was frightened by the latest generosity of the French. Sure, they'd been good neighbors, never playing their radio too loud or forgetting to take in their trash cans, but this most recent gift was too much: today French Kiss lost to Italia. Christmas in Fremantle, French style.

We were guaranteed either second or third place, regardless of how we fared against New Zealand. The fourth-place finisher would race New Zealand in the semi-finals. Now French Kiss owned that spot. I was tempted to lend them a sleeve of 1,200-grit sandpaper to speed up their craft. They were going to need a dolphin strapped to their keel or a pair of Detroit diesels under the floorboards to punch through the New Zealand craft.

New Zealand proved it again today, in this final showdown. We didn't race poorly, a little fatigued perhaps, but all our crew maneuvers went well. The Kiwis worked ahead on the start, but only by a few feet. Rounding the first mark, we were barely fifteen seconds behind. Against anyone but New Zealand that small margin would have been chump change. But the Kiwis' experience at being ahead, and staying between the opposition and the next mark or the finish line, was supreme. We had the outside lane the whole afternoon. All told, we might have sailed an extra two hundred yards. New Zealand beat us by fifty-nine seconds.

After hanging the sails to dry, I rode my bike to the media center to have a look at a rare sight: all the Challenging skippers had been invited to the press conference. For most of these skippers, this was the last America's Cup press conference they were likely to attend, at least for the next three or four years. Only two of the skippers really looked the part, our own Tom Blackaller and Italia's Mauro Pelaschier. The others looked like sunburned tourists anxious to get back to their hotel rooms and crack open a beer.

Blacky and Mauro were in no hurry to duck the limelight. Mauro was the only skipper, practically the only sailor competing, with a beard. Sitting next to his conservative counterparts Mauro looked like a reincarnation of Melville's Ahab. A reporter asked Mauro if he would return in 1991. He slowly shook his head, as though to say, 'I just went through three months of hell and you want to talk about doing it again?' Mauro glanced around for a second, looking for a harpoon with which to skewer the reporter.

Blacky looked especially happy under the bright lights, silver-haired, tanned and tired but not defeated. Blacky fielded more questions than the other skippers combined, and at exactly the right moment he made a dramatic offering to New Zealand skipper Chris Dickson—a check for $5,000.

(Earlier today a mystery man had walked down the dock and said to Blacky, "I'll cover that $5,000 bet." True to his word, the man wrote out a check for $5,000 to cover a bet that was already lost. I found out later that this man was a former commodore of the St. Francis Yacht Club.)

For the first time Dickson snapped out of his weird trance and accepted the check from Blacky like a kid getting $10 from his kooky uncle at Christmas.

The wager had now been paid in full. We would start fresh on December 28. USA versus Stars and Stripes. Best four out of seven races.

43
Christmas, Alive in Freo

The weather felt more like the Fourth of July than Christmas. The temperature had crawled into the 40-degree range earlier this week, which translated into 100+ US-style degrees. Popular down-under Christmas gifts were a pair of shorts or sunglasses or a twelve-pack of nice cold Black Swan beer. Our simple needs had already been satisfied: we had our place in the semi-finals, and we didn't have to race the Kiwis. Nice.

Christmas was definitely more fun back home. I missed Christmas tree lots—no trees over three feet high grew in this part of the country. Fortunately, the natives had absolutely no idea what they were missing. *Peanuts* television specials never graced their holiday TV screens. The Salvation Army was fighting its war somewhere else.

The Christmas trees and television specials were missing, but the spirit of Christmas was here, alive and well. We had a yacht race yesterday—not in 12-meters and not with rock star sailors. These yachts were strictly of the cruising variety, and the sailors were handicapped children. A few crewmen from our syndicate, Sheik, Dana Timmer, and I, plus a crewman from Azzurra, came along for the ride. The kids owned the day.

These kids had a sad array of disabilities, but as soon as we left the dock the problems shrank to small proportions. One young woman, completely blind, sat in the very bow of my boat, the sun and wind caressing her face the whole time we were out to sea. She drank the pleasure of the moment like the finest wine. She never stopped smiling. Christmas, alive and well in Fremantle.

44
Boxing Day

In Australia, the day after Christmas is called Boxing Day. Boxing Day comes from an old English tradition in which folks boxed up their extra food and gave it to the needy.

Our modest syndicate was not exactly destitute, but nonetheless we did receive some extremely nice gifts from our wealthy, now retired neighbors. For example, we found a mint-condition carbon-fiber boom on our doorstep—a gift from America II. This boom weighed about fifty pounds less than our old, now extinct boom, and by saving that awesome amount of weight we hoped to be even more competitive in light winds.

The Canadian brotherhood slipped a matching set of carbon-fiber spreaders under our door. The spreaders would lighten the load on our mast by another twenty pounds. Any weight saved on the mast would help us sail more upright, and that translated into being able to point higher into the wind.

Heart of America gave us a spinnaker pole, but not an ordinary Sears mail order pole. This was a classy Neiman Marcus sectionalized spinnaker pole that must have cost them fifty head of cattle. Our new pole would live below decks and see the light of day only if we should break our regular spinnaker pole.

The Eagle connection gave us a generous bouquet of sails, but I wished they had included the receipt so we could return the sails to the store where they were purchased. It was a nice gesture. As a special gift we also received the use of the Eagle's athletic bowman, Mike Pentecost, who could take over for Dana Timmer if Dana needed a break. (Scott Inveen had been relegated to permanent shore patrol.)

There is always one gift you really want but don't receive. In this case I really wanted Shadow. America II had a ferocious German shepherd guard dog named Shadow, a virtual biting legend around Fremantle. They certainly wouldn't need him anymore. Shadow's nickname was Chainsaw, and he had been known to chew through five layers of Kevlar to get to a nosy reporter. In the old days at the America II compound, the guard would lock himself into the toolshed at night and let Shadow have the run of the place. At daybreak a net was thrown over Shadow and he was given a Tasty Vittles sedative.

We received one unexpected gift—three cases of Budweiser beer from Stars and Stripes. What? Why? A trick? Better let Blackaller sample the beer first. Was this some weird psychological ploy to take the edge off our fighting spirit? We meditated over the possibilities while powering through the first dozen beers. The whole team gathered around the garage door of the sail loft, kicking at the spent casings that littered the ground and discussing possible motives behind the free Bud. What was crafty Dennis Conner up to? We knew he had arranged for a special machine to be flown from San Diego to measure the wall thickness of the Kiwi 12-meter. Perhaps he had stopped by the 7-Eleven when he was home.

The second case brought out the funny stories—about the time someone accidentally hooked up the spinnaker so that it came out of the hatch sideways. Fortunately, this happened during a practice when no photographers were around.

The third case of Bud was for toasting the future: the Cup, Alan Bond, overrides, Oz, longboarding; bench press contests, Ron Anderson, Traci Lords, Fred of Fred's Place. The gifts I had received through this long campaign were good friends and a knowledge of sailing and its wildness that very few people understood. Now if only we could win that damn Cup.

45
Semi-final 1
Slam Dunking Against Stars and Stripes

A previously obscure nautical term was given great play at this America's Cup: the slam dunk. A dunk takes place on the upwind legs when the boats are converging on opposite tacks. The lead boat, as soon as it crosses the other boat, tacks, or slam dunks, on the face of her opposition. If done correctly, the dunker will position himself directly on top of the dunkee. The victim of the slam dunk is forced to sail underneath the lead boat, getting bad air and generally having a miserable time.

Slam dunking is like someone cutting in front of you in the checkout line at the supermarket. Slam dunking says, 'In your face, buddy. Take my stern and shove it.' A well-placed slam dunk will stifle any progress by the opposition. When it doesn't work, when the trailing boat has enough speed to scoot around the dunker, and the slam dunker is left in his opponent's wake.

The local helicopter pilots were finally making some decent money as a dozen helicopters puttered overhead throughout the race. The spectator boats overflowed with passengers, but not too many of these spectators were interested in Kiwi Magic versus French Kiss. That race was over by the first windward mark with only one interesting occurrence: French Kiss was flying a protest flag before she had even left the dock. The French were protesting the Kiwis for being too fast, via fiberglass, and for generally taking the fun out of the sport.

Everyone had come to see our little tussle: California State Championships, Dennis Connor versus Tom Blackaller.

No one was disappointed by the fight.

It went the full fifteen rounds, knockdown, drag out. For the first 22 miles, Conner was never more than two lengths behind us. Imagine a 60,000 pound dinosaur chasing you down the freeway for three hours.

A few funny moments were mixed in with the oaths and cursing and frazzled nerves. Once we tacked unbelievably close to Dennis when we didn't have the right-of-way. He sidled up next to us, like a chunky bully in Danny's Bar down on Chestnut Street. Our beast was about ten feet to leeward of the Stars and Stripes—amazingly close. Naturally everyone felt obligated to say something, and in this case the tactician on Stars and Stripes took the initiative: "Did you have mast line at the last mark rounding?" he asked.

Cayard, somewhat confused, said, "Ah, yes, I think we had mast line."

"Okay," the tactician said, "then we're protesting you because we don't think you did."

Their red protest flag was immediately hoisted, the punch line to a vaguely funny joke.

As we all expected, the race came down to the last windward leg. We rounded the mark about a length ahead and immediately went toward the right side of the course. Dennis went for the left side and then tacked. We matched his tack with one of our own, and then our whole crew started chanting, "Slam dunk, slam dunk."

Blacky had slam dunk written all over his face. This would be it, the final blow. We crossed in the lead and then tacked on his bow—classic slam-dunk posturing. But Blacky suddenly realized he might have cut it just a shade too close. Dennis swung his bow around and tried to smash our stern, a completely legal move that, if successful, would have won him the race because at that moment D.C. had the right-of-way. To avoid being tagged we had to tack again, before we were up to speed, and suddenly Dennis had the upper hand.

This was all a bit confusing—only Russ Silvestri understood all the nuances—but the bottom line was that Conner and company now had the lead and the favored side of the course. We were left to play catch-up the rest of the race. We didn't catch up, and the first race of the semi-finals went to Stars and Stripes by ten seconds.

Tomorrow, December 29, would be another slam-dunking day.

46
Semi-final 2

When the second semi-final was over, the whole sailing crew eased into Blacky's office for the requisite team meeting. No one talked as we waited for Blacky to say something. He was carefully studying some papers, a rule book perhaps, to decide if he should go ahead with his protest of Conner for *un-seamanlike conduct*.

Blacky adjusted his reading glasses a little. Finally he raised his head and said, "Well, it says on this telex that the Rams lost to the Redskins. New York beat Kansas City."

No, we were not dead—wounded a little, a scratch, a flesh wound. Yes, it hurt. Now we had to win a few races, exactly as we had done in the past. The prospect of achieving this goal had seemed completely within our grasp that morning. Now I was a little worried.

Yacht racing is a funny game. Imagine our opponent being over the starting line early, as was Stars and Stripes. Naturally we should have stomped them into submission.

Instead, Conner found a massive wind shift only moments after re-crossing the starting line and within five minutes our relative position had shifted from lengths ahead to lengths behind. As navigator Craig Healy said so appropriately at the time, "Ah, we might be able to cross him if we tacked, but I doubt it."

That wind shift cost us about six lengths, with Stars and Stripes making up the starting line deficit and then rounding the first mark three lengths ahead of us.

We had a good run down to the leeward mark, at times so close to Conner that some of our crew screamed all sorts of unflattering nonsense his way. How many wind shifts did we miss while concentrating on the girth of Conner's behind? A tornado of hot wind blew from the mouths of our more vocal crewmen, and always to our detriment.

The bottom line was all that mattered: Stars and Stripes rounded the first leeward mark a length ahead, and equally important, they held the coveted inside position. Conner took off for the favored right side of the course, and we immediately tacked left, in search of clean, fresh, unsullied air. Waiting for us, a half-mile away, was another thirty-degree wind shift—a header of the worst variety—and that stuffed us back another six lengths. We played follow the leader the rest of the way around the course. The final margin showed us losing by a whopping 3:02.

For me the afternoon's highlight was when Blacky allowed me to sail the USA back to the harbor. Cayard sat in the very aft part of the cockpit, eyes closed, trying to sort through the jumbled tactical decisions he had made throughout the long afternoon. Cayard didn't want to drive. Blacky was taking a stroll on the foredeck, inspecting the mast and boom fittings, looking at nothing in particular. No one was too talkative. I felt as though we were sailing to Madagascar and not Fremantle Harbor.

Despite the loss, I reveled in this truly rare occurrence—a lowly grinder driving a 12-meter. The wheel had a nice leather grip, and my fingers fit snugly around the circumference. This was no puny go-cart steering wheel; this wheel was huge, and I had to use my weight to make it turn. The driving felt good, a tough, satisfying motion leaning into a turn and a second later feeling our 60,000-pound beast respond with a groan. We lost the race, but we beat Stars and Stripes back to the harbor. Still, I was worried.

47
Semi-final 3

In exactly one hour we would have the most crucial race of our lives. Naturally we had a thousand pre-race preparations to complete before we could leave the dock. But first, by order of Blacky's secretary, the whole USA syndicate had to convene next to the equipment trailer for the team picture. For about ten minutes we stood next to the trailer, laughing, goofing, stamping the ground, waiting for shutters to click. Our little fraternity had grown over the year to about 30 members including shore patrol. This was a small tribe compared to Kookaburra with their 125 paid employees, but still we were large enough to require three rows of sailors and workers to fit within camera range.

The professional photographer who had been hired for the occasion directed us to scrunch together in tight formation.

Finally we settled into the proper team-picture pattern, short guys in the front, cool guys in the middle row, cooler guys in the back row with sunglasses and hats: Okay, everybody, say *Beat Conner.*

"Hey, wait a second," Sharon, the photographer, said. "Someone's missing."

Along with being a top photog (and one of our skipper's former girlfriends), Sharon was also a sharp-eyed observer. Yes, someone was missing: Thomas D. Blackaller, Jr.

"Ah, to hell with him," Cayard said. "Take the fucking picture. We're running late."

Like a scene from a good comedy, as soon as the final picture was snapped Blackaller came charging through the compound gates wearing his Henri-Lloyd jacket and saying, "Okay, I'm here. Let's do the picture now."

"Sorry, Chief," Cayard said. "We already took the team pic."

We were, in fact, into the early stages of dispersal, shedding our jackets to counter the morning sun. I sensed that Blackaller was not going to let the moment pass. His initial response of "Fuck that" confirmed my suspicions. On hearing these words, we turned our heads in the direction of the two sailing warriors. The young buck and the grizzled veteran were about to knock antlers. Cayard and Blacky eyed each other for a second, waiting for that slight smile that says "No worries, Mate, this is just a joke, and everything will be right in a blink." But no smile showed on either face. No more sparring—they went right for the jugular.

Blacky erupted first: "What the fuck are you doing taking the team picture without me? What the fuck's going on here? Who said to go ahead and take the picture without me? Who said it? I've got to know."

"You knew what time to be here," Cayard said.

"Listen, Cayard, you wouldn't be here if it wasn't for me. This compound wouldn't be here if I hadn't raised the money."

"Isn't this just like Christmas Day, when you told J.T. not to wait for the other guys who wanted to visit the aircraft carrier? You knew the time."

"Fuck you, Cayard, I raised $8 million for this syndicate, and if you think we're going to take the team picture without me, you can shove it up."

This little repartee went on for five minutes, and by the end the whole team was wondering if we'd ever go racing. Fortunately for posterity, the whole shouting match was recorded by two television crews, one from Seattle and the ESPN crew who happened to be recording a joyous New Year's message. An unedited videocassette of their dust-up could become a big hit if properly marketed.

Finally a truce was called and the camera was reloaded with fresh film. The new and proper picture was snapped with a slightly overheated Blacky in the front row. Nine months later I was given the opportunity to buy a team picture. Two different pictures were offered for sale. Neither picture included Blackaller, but in both images the French Kiss logo from the neighboring compound was clearly shown in the background.

We survived that fun and a short time later went yacht racing. Just before the start I glanced over to the Sourdough and noticed one passenger leaning over the railing at a curious angle, as though she were admiring her reflection in the bumpy, rolling water.

"Looks like Dana Timmer's girlfriend is a little seasick," I said.

"No," Russ corrected, "it's Blackaller's daughter, Brooke."

Yes, one of Blacky's two daughters was grasping the rail, feet braced, casting her gaze downward. No doubt she was regretting having eaten that second helping of cheese-bread for breakfast, or more likely she was cursing having ever stepped onto the Sourdough. Like tea leaves in a cup, her now unwanted breakfast filtering through the waves could have been deciphered to portend our future: we had another long day ahead of us.

At last the ten-minute gun sounded and we could get to racing. The spectator boats were chock-full of passengers, and when we ranged within a hundred feet they screamed like Romans at a Christians vs. lions matchup. They wanted blood, masts breaking, men overboard. They yelled, "Go, Tom, knock 'em dead," with such abandon that I couldn't help feeling even more inspired. Unfortunately, a lack of inspiration wasn't our problem. We needed more boat speed, or a more clever afterguard, or stronger grinders, or we simply didn't have our act together.

Conner and crew motored around the course as though they had an engine attached beneath the hull instead of a pair of lead wings. We did little more than watch in admiration. Blacky frequently smiled, grimaced, and looked serious for the newly installed on-board camera. He seemed resigned to losing. We lost by two minutes.

We had one short-lived ray of hope. Late in the evening we received word from ESPN commentator Gary Jobson that the Stars and Stripes had been inspected after the race and was found to be sitting below her marks. Our spirits buoyed for a few short minutes, but nothing more came of it. Jobson must have been mistaken, or maybe Conner sponged the bilge until his boat floated correctly on its marks. For whatever reasons, they passed a second inspection. Now we had to win four races in a row. I'd settle for one.

48
Semi-final 4

I spent all morning looking for good omens—maybe a new freighter in the harbor named Super Comeback. Imagine the headlines if we won four straight: USA Wins in Wild Upset. Conner Last Seen Hitchhiking to Ayers Rock. Crew of USA Goes on to Win the America's Cup after Previously Unknown Grinder Wrests Wheel from Blackaller and Drives USA to Victory.

The mood off the dock was subdued and that worried me. What happened to our usual boisterous cursing and oaths and general pre-race unruly behavior? I just couldn't believe we had forgotten how to curse over the past two days. But maybe that was a good omen—trying something different for a change.

Our two most loyal fans, the Modesto Kids—Ken Miller and Kevin Gray from Modesto, California—hitched a ride on the Sourdough to watch the race, and that was a great omen. These two teenagers had been living in the abandoned generator shed behind our machine shop for the past month, and gradually they had been adopted as our in-house groupies. Having them close at hand during the race would certainly be a plus.

Our forever-loyal sailmakers were still hard at work in the loft when we left the dock. Olga was sewing a new jib bag, and Chewy had his scissors in gear, trimming a few unwanted inches off a new mainsail. That was a good omen because sailmakers are practical folk, and they wouldn't be working unless they thought we had more races to come.

For an hour it looked as though the race might be postponed until the next day. Cayard's wife, Eika, made use of the delay by donning her skimpiest bikini and settling into a high-powered tanning session on the foredeck of Trojan Lady. Eika wasn't worried—win, lose, or postpone, she had seventy-eight degrees, crystal-clear sky, pure green water. Compared with snow-bound Stockholm, nothing could top this life.

Eventually the wind turned around, and within five minutes the breeze grew from zero to twenty knots. The fault in the wind machine had been fixed, and now we had plenty of wind to act out this final scene.

But what about the race—the actual race? The race was almost identical to the first race, except we were behind and chomping at Conner's heels. On the third beat Cayard found a wind shift—a lift—that we desperately needed, and the USA appeared to nudge ahead of Stars and Stripes for the first time all day. A minute later Blacky tacked and now—finally—that infinitesimal moment of truth had arrived. The bull was charging towards us. But we had the right-of-way. We could make our slight lead stick if we slam dunked on his face. At the crucial instant Blacky slam dunked, and Conner was forced to dip underneath us. But Conner is the undisputed master of wiggling out of uncompromising slam-dunking positions, and he managed to slide his Stars and Stripes far enough underneath that we received his bad air.

Blacky tacked to get clean air, and Conner strode away on his Stars and Stripes like a chunky jockey, now owning the preferred side of the course. We never had another chance. The door was closed. Our chance at victory had come and gone. The window slammed on our fingers. We lost.

"Well," Blacky said, as he gave me the obligatory final handshake as he was leaving the compound, "I guess this means we have to get real jobs."

When Blacky reached out for the hand of Stevie Erickson, Stevie pulled back and said, "I don't want a handshake. I want my half-model."

We had all been promised a half-model of the USA. No half-model ever arrived in the mail.

The Modesto Kids had gone legit. No longer were they ordinary groupies. Overnight they had become press pass carrying reporters for the Turlock Journal. Kevin told me the late edition was being held until he filed his story. No doubt they'd want to move out of our old shed and into the sail loft. We had plenty of room.

For the 12-meter USA from the St. Francis Yacht Club, the party was over.

49
One Last Look

Big Mike Erlin and I drove to Nordic Fitness to return the weightlifting equipment we had rented four months ago. After dropping off the bench presses, squat rack, incline press, and various implements of weight room torture, we drove home along the Swan River. A dozen quick little sailboats called Aussie 18s skimmed across the water faster than any 12-meter could ever muster. Fast as they were, Aussie 18s lacked something I had grown to love: the unwieldy grace and brute power of a monster 12-meter.

Too bad we didn't win the Cup so that the people of San Francisco could enjoy seeing the 12-meters dance and parry during the next America's Cup celebration.

On the way back to the compound we passed the Swan River Brewery (abandoned) and the cricket oval (not abandoned), a pure green gem set next to the river.

Mike suggested we make a quick detour to the Royal Perth Yacht Club for one last look at the America's Cup. Our clothes didn't match the yacht club's civilized decor (we were not even wearing USA T-shirts), but the security guard took mercy on us after I told him this was our last day in Western Australia. This was not quite true, but what the hell.

"Okay, you can see the Cup," he said. "But you'll need to be quiet—a television crew is filming right now."

"No worries, Mate," I said.

We walked upstairs to the trophy room and immediately saw a man on his knees about two feet in front of the glass trophy case, peering through the viewfinder on his camera. He looked as though he was praying to the God of Yachting, the 100 Guinea Cup—the America's Cup. That strange piece of antique silverwork had caused more excitement and disappointment and pure unadulterated fun than I had ever dreamed possible.

The cameraman's lights bore down on the Cup, making it shine and weave, reflecting a hypnotizing glow. I thought of all the exciting times I'd had over the last year, bouncing over the waves or, more accurately, through the waves, with awesome, powerful abandon. The races, both wins and losses, rivaled the Olympics for pure exhilaration. Some of the best times were those we enjoyed off the water: when we wet-sanded the Geek way back in September and Mike started singing *Swing Low Sweet Chariot*. The whole sanding crew started singing, and we didn't stop for an hour. How often can you sing with your mates these days? We shared the rarest and best of times.

Our star had burned like hell for a short time. We had looked so clever and innovative with our two rudders, the Geek, and our haughty all-star crew. I thought we knew what we were doing on the race course, but in the last four races we had looked very ordinary. That is simply the way it goes sometimes.

I loved this adventure, except for those two Kenny volcanoes directed at me. I learned a whole new language—

the language of sailing. I didn't know a spinnaker from a short sheet when I started. Now I can call myself a sailor, a fine title to own. I'd made the best possible friends through this arduous experience, and that I valued more than any other aspect.

50
Stars and Stripes vs. Kookaburra

I have no idea where I was during the New Zealand vs. Stars and Stripes series that immediately followed our debacle. I might have gone to Bali, but I can't be sure. I do know that I bought a sailboard, a surfboard, and a boogie board, and I used them every day until I felt myself growing gills. My interest in the Cup resurfaced just in time for the finals, Stars and Stripes vs. Kookaburra.

Final 1

Madness in Freo. New arrivals were pouring into Fremantle. The crowd that had been predicted for October, and hoped for by the merchants for three long years, had finally arrived. There was a twenty-minute wait at the McDonalds as the line stretched out the door and onto the sidewalk. The tourist assault was here in full force.

The breakwater leading from the harbor to the ocean was crammed with cheering Australians, thirty thousand people, a third of them intoxicated, at 9:30 a.m. People climbed onto the roofs of buildings for a better view, thousands of flags waved, kids sat on their dads' shoulders. Everyone was there to see and cheer the Kookaburra crew. Not even the Pope drew this kind of adulation when he had visited Western Australia a few weeks earlier.

This was not the usual Aussie style according to my Australia IV grinder friend, Andy Cannon. "Ninety, no ninety-five percent of Australians," Andy told me, "don't know the words to our national anthem."

The remaining members of the USA crew piled onto the Trojan Lady tender to watch this first contest. We flew a *privileged spectator* flag from our antenna, which allowed us to be close to the action. I felt very uneasy to be watching and not competing. It was not a particularly pleasant sensation.

As Stars and Stripes sailed close to our tender, Scott Easom noticed that they were using a USA mainsail. The sail was our newest #10, designed for light winds, and I remembered heaving it into the back of a Stars and Stripes pickup truck soon after we were eliminated. Our sail must have been to their liking, because when the race was delayed because a new and stronger wind was predicted, Conner chose not to change his mainsail. Kookaburra's skipper, Iain Murray, however, used the delay to change to a heavier #20 mainsail, and that may have been part of his undoing. (I eventually learned that we sold our #10 mainsail to Stars and Stripes. We did not loan it as I had first assumed.)

The start was even, with Conner going to the left side of the course and Murray going right. A minute into the race Conner hooked into a twenty-degree wind shift that powered him to a three-length lead at their first crossing. Stars and Stripes never looked back the rest of the afternoon.

Conner likened the light winds and spectator chop to Newport, Rhode Island, and not the infamous Gage Roads, Fremantle Doctor terrain. Except for a few puffs, the wind never left the #10 range. Today's weather was something special. The number of times the wind had not built throughout the afternoon could be counted on one hand. Murray's weatherman predicted the usual increasing wind weather pattern, and Kookaburra was saddled with the wrong mainsail.

Conner had been acknowledged as having excellent heavy wind speed, but now his ability in light winds had also been revealed. The Fremantle merchants were wringing their hands at the thought of a quick and deadly series.

Final 2

The Doctor came home with a vengeance today, and Conner was ready. The start went off in twenty-two knots of breeze and built to twenty-six knots as the race progressed. Conner worked these conditions like an artist, and he led Murray at every mark. Stars and Stripes put to rest the rumor that Kookaburra was superior on the downwind legs.

Conner was a master at *scalloping*. He carved his boat upwind between the waves and then fell off in the bumpy water. The net gain is that he sailed a shade higher and closer to the mark without losing much speed.

After Stars and Stripes returned to dock and the boat was tucked away for the night, Conner made a formal presentation to each of his crewmen: a Rolex watch. This was part of their bounty for winning the right to represent the America's Cup challengers. During the presentation Conner recognized each crewman. He also singled out my friend Tom Darling, an 1984 Olympic silver medalist in the eight-oared shell.

"Tom is a winner of an Olympic gold medal," Conner said. "No? Oh, right, he won the silver medal. Well, Tom, consider this your gold medal."

Conner also singled out crewman John MacCausland. John was a rare breed on Stars and Stripes—he was a self-admitted *mushroom*. The crew of Stars and Stripes 85, the tune-up boat for Stars and Stripes 87, had their own distinctive banner: a six-foot mushroom that hung from the forestay. John MacCausland, a charter member of the mushroom squad, explained the meaning behind the banner: "We're always kept in the dark, they feed us bullshit, and somebody is always stepping on us."

Final 3

Rather than call a *lay day* after their second defeat, Murray and company surprised everyone by deciding to race straight away. Kookaburra had been defeated in light winds and in heavy winds. Medium winds were predicted for the third contest, and they hoped their speed would finally show through.

Sure enough, medium winds held throughout the day, and so did Conner's lead. On the first downwind leg Stars and Stripes slipped forty-two seconds ahead of Kookaburra. As in the whole final series, the Stars and Stripes crew maintained flawless execution of every spinnaker set and takedown. With simple, unadulterated superior boat speed, Conner was looking like a yachting genius.

A bomb scare broke up an otherwise predictable afternoon on Gage Roads. Later at a press conference Iain Murray said, "We took the option after the bomb scare to continue the race because, as we were well behind, if the bomb went off it wasn't going to affect the result of the race."

By now the results were no longer full-page news in the local West Australian newspaper. The crowd at McDonalds had thinned out. A few tentative *Clearance Sale* signs were showing at the souvenir stands around town, except for Stars and Stripes merchandise. That stuff was selling at a premium.

The problem with this sport, Murray and company would agree, is that year-in year-out hard work will not necessarily pay off in boat speed. Boat design is so critical that no matter how strong your grinders or how clever your tactician, a boat with superior boat speed will win the race. The America's Cup is a damn frustrating sport.

Final 4

A huge Aussie crowd was again on the jetty, cheering their heroes, flags waving, urging on Murray and crew. When Conner passed, they clapped and showed respect for the man who was about to wrench the Cup out of their hands.

The America's Cup and Australia were such a fine combination. Australia used it like a new deity. They need the Cup like Boston needs the Celtics, only a hundred times more.

Walter Cronkite was on the Stars and Stripes dock when they departed, and he had a few thoughts on the impending race: "By 4:20 this afternoon Conner will be wearing the crown again—now all he has to do is defend it for the next 132 years. The predicted conditions today are the same as Monday, so he really shouldn't have that much difficulty. Maybe something happened in the Kookaburra camp over the last forty-eight hours, but I can't imagine what it could be."

The race, as Cronkite predicted, was a parade, with Conner playing the zinc oxide-covered grand marshal. No furious tacking duel was led by Kookaburra for one simple reason. Conner never bothered to respond to that sort of provocation. Once ahead, Stars and Stripes sailed for the wind shifts, and Conner paid little notice to what his opponent was doing.

The fourth and final victory, the America's Cup, the ultimate retribution for his 1983 disaster, went to Dennis Conner and Stars and Stripes.

I stood on the Stars and Stripes dock with my tape recorder catching the mood after the winners returned: an enormous American flag was flying from the Stars and Stripes backstay— a huge flag, big enough to cover a house.

Everyone was going for the big swim. An uninvited guest jumped over the fence, and the guards corralled him right away. Syndicate leader Malin Burnham was surrounded by a dozen cameras and reporters. Serious looking uniformed guards were leading their guard dogs along the compound perimeter. Stars and Stripes design team Britt Chance and Dave Pedric were looking for someone to throw in. The Travelift was bringing up Stars and Stripes. Jimmy Buffet was walking around, soaking wet with a beer in hand. Champagne everywhere. Boats were parading in front of the dock, watching the fun. Everyone was crowded around the stern of the Betsy, Stars and Stripes tender. There was about a ten-foot gap between the stern and the dock—the throw-in pool. The Travelift was driving Stars and Stripes onto the hard—one crewman was standing on board—he grabbed the ensign and was waving it over his head. It was no match for the huge flag overhead. Reporters grabbed at the shroud that covered the keel, getting their first look at the winning keel. The Beach Boys *Surfin' USA* was playing over the loudspeakers.

As I left the Stars and Stripes compound, I saw Kookaburra port grinder Rick Goodrich walking down Mews Avenue, the street that encircled most of the syndicate compounds. Rick was still wearing his distinctive headband and sailing gear. He looked a foot taller than the rest of the crowd as he made his way down the sidewalk. Here was a real live 12-meter sailor. They had watched him on television for weeks, and now he was among them. Rick carried his Aigle sea boots in his left hand, and when he saw a trash bin on the opposite side of the street he made straight for it. He lifted the lid and with barely a one-second hesitation—to think of all the miles his boots had served him, of all the work and time invested, the dream not quite realized—he dumped the boots in the trash bin. Then he walked to the Stars and Stripes compound to congratulate his American counterpart and wish him the best of luck.

Epilogue: Going Walkabout

While Dennis Conner and crew drove through downtown Manhattan in a blizzard of ticker tape, I quietly drove away from Fremantle. My battered Holden panel van slowly picked up speed as I entered the first miles of the Nullarbor Plain.

I was seeing Australia the hard way, driving from Fremantle to Sydney and then up to Cairns. I had my credit card, a bag of Crunchy Cheetos, and a cassette of Janis Joplin's greatest hits. In Aussie terms, I was going walkabout. Bring on the Nullarbor.

Nullarbor Plain. The Nullarbor. The scorching, arid, deadly Nullarbor. Say it slow, hang on the syllables, let them roll off your tongue: Null is no, none, vacant lot, no services. Arbor is trees, shrubs, vines, plantation, ranch. Put them together and you have a messy Latin translation for Acres of Nothing.

I had been passionately warned against crossing the Nullarbor, mainly by people who had never done it.

"Take the train," my friend behind the counter at the Midget Deli said. "Or a bus or fly."

"Listen," I told her, "nobody walks in L.A. or rides the bus either. We drive."

So this was the Nullarbor. It reminded me of driving from Los Angeles to Las Vegas, except that it took forever. While cruising all day under a shocking-blue sky, I saw only thirty cars coming toward me. Lousy place for a McDonalds. Very few gas stations had taken root in the desert. A big dot on the map that intuitively promised a 7- Eleven, Ramada Inn, and Safeway turned out to be nothing more than a few dusty trailers. One trailer was always reserved for the bar. Another trailer was the hotel, a legal necessity in Australia since a bar must be linked to a hotel, and the third trailer was the gas station. The gas station attendant could always be found in the bar.

I quickly perfected the Nullarbor Wave: simply raise the forefinger of the hand that was resting on the steering wheel, and like magic the opposing driver would do the same thing. Total time: half a second; total calories: .001. Efficient, studied, controlled, the Nullarbor Wave symbolized what this desert was about—conserving energy.

But the cyclists earned an unabashed thumbs-up. I saw three bicyclists pedaling across the Nullarbor, all of whom appeared to be Japanese. I hoped they had studied the scale of the map they were using.

As the light faded, I began to test the zipper effect driving along Eyre Highway between Balladonia and Eucla. Miles of emptiness . No cars, nothing. Cruising at 110 kilometers an hour with darkness taking over and only a slight glow fading in the rearview mirror, I put the car exactly in the middle of the road, tires straddling the center stripe. Then I turned out the lights. At first I slipped into a nice floating sensation, lost in space, and then the zipper effect took over: the road seemed to open or unzip, behind the car. If I were to stop and go in reverse, I'd fall into a cavern so deep I might never touch bottom. So I just kept driving, and when I couldn't take any more, I waited just one more second. Then I turned on the lights.

Driving across the Nullarbor that first night, I realized that I missed my friends, Dana Timmer, Russ Silvestri, and Bruce Epke–pretty much everyone on the team. Maybe we'd meet again at the next America's Cup.

A few random grinder-sailor terms

Afterguard: skipper, navigator, tactician. Some crews used the derogatory term blackcoats. When a member of the afterguard skips the work and only sails, he is called a *rock star*.

Andy Allen: machinist/boardsailor/great guy. He joined us late in Australia. We needed him to bring another rudder from San Francisco, and Andy also decided to bring his sailboards. The airline's charge for the extra freight—the rudder—was $5,000.

America's Cup: the original prize was called the *R.Y.S.* *£100 Cup* (Royal Yacht Squadron 100 Guinea Cup). The first yacht to win this Cup in 1851 was called *America*. The cup was then re-named America's Cup. For the Fremantle competition, the New York Yacht Club christened its entry America II, so that it would be the second yacht named *America* to reclaim the Cup. Good name. Not a great yacht.

Bald-headed: going around a mark without the jib up.

Barking: going slow, using the standard dog-reference common to sailing.

Blue Light Café: popular bar with our team in San Francisco's marina district. Our bowman, Scott Inveen, met his future bride, Pamela Pew, when she served him a beer in the Blue Light's crowded confines.

Bogs: Aussie Hell's Angels. They roamed Fremantle before the Cup, and I'm sure they have reclaimed their territory now that we are gone.

Conn Findlay: the greatest waterman in the history the world. Conn is my rowing hero. He won two Olympic gold medals in the pair-with coxswain event. Conn also crewed on several winning America's Cup yachts. He helped our syndicate get organized in Fremantle. A true champion.

Golden octopus: an extremely bad override that occurred during a tack as the trimmer hauled in the jib line. The usual clean, even wraps of jib line around the drum are replaced with a twisted, knotted, horrible knot that cinches so tight the jib can neither be drawn closer nor let free. Break out the wire cutters. In a close race, an override is disaster.

Hauling the mail: going fast. Hold tight.

Just like Perth: Hank Stuart's favorite saying, first introduced on a windy day in San Francisco. He'd shout it out at least once an hour, regardless of the wind conditions. Even in Perth he could not go a day without chanting his mantra.

Keelco: an outfit in Long Beach that constructs the keels for most of the 12-meters made in the United States.

The company has a secret formula for making a heavier flavor of lead.

Kevlar: a bright yellow fabric, tough, used for making sails and bulletproof vests. After a few weeks of Fremantle abuse the material slowly turned ugly brown and then self-destructed.

Mary's office: code name for our compound headquarters. Cayard would call Mary's office thirty minutes before the start of the race to get the latest weather conditions.

Lowell North: nicknamed the Pope. Lowell is the founder of North Sails. (Our sails were made in North's San Diego and Alameda lofts.) He knows everything about sailing. He has won every race. He is universally revered as the father of the modern yacht racing. Quiet man, reserved, classy.

Oz: Australia, one of the few countries where Americans are not hated.

Panties in a bunch (or *all bunched up*, or simply *bunched*): angry, mad, pissed, furious, as in *Look out. Kenny has his panties in a bunch.* This saying was used every day in regards to Kenny.

Parked: when a 12-meter appears stalled on the race course, especially after a tack. A too-quick tack can cause a yacht to lose momentum and appear to be dead in the water—parked.

Potato Patch: a hundred acres of the roughest water ii California, perfect for pre-Fremantle racing and only a mile from the Marin Headlands off San Francisco. The Patch's water was a jumbled mess of confused whitecap caused by shallowness of the area, the water streaming out the Golden Gate during ebb tide, the shearing wind pattern. Added together, an outing in the Potato Patel could knock your fillings loose.

Spank whitey: play golf.

12-meters: they are big, beautiful, heavy (downright obese, some experts claim), clumsy, expensive, picturesque. 12-meter boats are weird. Never in history has there been a stranger mating of high-tech design and ancient urges— the urge to go fast on the water. A 12-meter is a sailboat. A whole class of sailboats fall into the "meter" category—5.5-meter, 6-meter, 10-meter. The meter part of the name refers to the formula that defines this class of racer, and not the length of the boat. In practical terms a 12-meter is about 66 feet long. The mast is 92 feet high. The boat weighs 60,000 pounds. A huge mainsail and an even bigger jib power the boat.

No engine is on board, no head (bathroom), no kitchen except for a cooler in the back of the bus, no bunks, although the sails stowed below decks are comfortable for sleeping on the long tow out to the race course. The computer and various instruments, wind speed, boat speedometer, and wind direction, are powered by four 12-volt batteries.

All the usual stuff is left off: running lights, CF numbers, refrigerator full of beer. We did, however, have life jackets stowed below along with two anchors in order to meet the 12-meter requirements. The actual rule book defining a 12-meter is about an inch thick and so complicated you need a Ph.D. in naval engineering just to buy one—and all to do a little sailing and not even overnight. The boats cost a fortune because they are handmade. From the first line that's drawn on the designer's drafting board to the name being painted on the transom, the total beast is massaged by a thousand hands until it is a true 12-meter. Then you better hope it is fast.

Foreword

I met Brad Lewis some four years ago. I was working on a magazine article which became a book about a group of young American single-scullers who were trying to represent the United States in the 1984 Olympics. I had prepared myself quite carefully and thought I knew a good deal about this, the most physically demanding of all sports; I had the names of the various favorites, and I watched the final in Princeton with eager anticipation. In that race someone named Brad Lewis, whom I had never heard of, took an immense early lead, rowed brilliantly and lost out on the final few strokes. Who, I immediately asked, was Brad Lewis?

I soon found out. He was intelligent, driven, and original. He was also the unlikeliest of rowers. He was from California, not from the East. He had gone to Cal-Irvine, a school almost no one had heard of, rather than Harvard, Yale, or Penn. He was considered different, an outsider, very much a loner even in the world of rowing, where everyone is essentially a loner. He was also a man of exceptional talents and rare individualism. Almost all the other scullers had worked out together that winter and spring. Brad Lewis had chosen to stay home in Newport Beach, California, and row there, devising some of the most ingenious regimens imaginable in order to compensate for the lack of competition. He also was a man with an innate ability to do things to his standards and specifications; he was able to walk away from colleges, rowing programs, and coaches if he thought he was not being given adequate respect. Later that year, as he rowed in a double scull, he put a small bumper sticker on his shell which said, "Question Authority." He was eventually ordered by rowing authorities to remove the bumper sticker. The sticker came off, I noted, but the attitude never changed.

That spring he was offered a chance by the Olympic coaches to be a backup oarsman for the double and the quad. He pondered it briefly, decided he was better than most of the oarsmen selected, and decided to form his own challenge boat with a partner named Paul Enquist. Now he was perfectly cast: he was the outsider challenging the establishment. The two of them were, Lewis kept telling Enquist, nothing less than warriors. Lewis made a giant banner and on it he painted: "No One Beats Us." In the Olympic trials he and Enquist demolished the double chosen at the camp, and won a chance to row at the Olympics. That was victory number one. Together they went out to California, trained brilliantly, and then to almost everyone's surprise except their own, won a gold medal in the double sculls.

After the Olympics, Brad continued rowing for a while, making an assault on Henley that fell just short of a gold medal. He was also trying to write about sculling. I became something of a literary adviser, and the first thing that impressed me was that for someone who had never written before, who had never even served an apprenticeship, he wrote very well. He is a natural writer. He was also at loose ends in his life, a little old to be a sculler, with few challenges left for him there. Thus it did not surprise me when I heard that he was crewing on one of the boats preparing for the America's Cup. Nor did it surprise me when I picked up a copy of Sports Illustrated and saw an article on sailing by Brad.

This is his book on that challenge. I am not a sailor; like most Americans, I do not know the sport and can only marvel at the sheer beauty of a race between gifted crews on these stunning boats. But what makes this book so valuable is that Brad takes us inside that world; it is an event and a world seen through the eyes of a man who is experienced at life, and yet a novice in this world. The eye is fresh and nothing is taken for granted. He misses none of the tension and confrontation which mark the sport. His is a wonderful view of the clash of egos of the men who command, and his account confirms my own belief that millionaires they may be, but in their hearts they are still essentially pirates. He explains not just the tactics and struggle involved but gives a feeling for the daily life as his boat, USA, prepares for the ultimate challenge. There is an additional benefit: Brad Lewis, Olympic gold medal winner, novice sailor, is a very good writer. In this book it comes through all the time—lovely little phrases (vanity license plates, he notes, are the "haiku of California"), a good ear, and a good sense of character. I think you will enjoy the sail to Australia with him.

David Halberstam
February, 1988

Made in the USA
Middletown, DE
07 December 2020

26448289R00135